The Strategy Gap

The
Strategy Gap

Leveraging Technology to Execute Winning Strategies

Michael Coveney
Dennis Ganster
Brian Hartlen
Dave King, Ph.D.

WILEY

John Wiley & Sons, Inc.

Library of Congress Cataloging-in-Publication Data:
The strategy gap : leveraging technology to execute winning strategies / by Michael Coveney . . . [et al.].
        p. cm.
Includes index.
    ISBN 0-471-21450-7 (cloth : alk. paper)
  1. Strategic planning.   2.   Management information systems.   3.
Decision support systems.   4.   Industrial management--Data processing.
I.   Coveney, Michael.
HD30.28.S7385 2003
658.4'012--dc21

                    2002015558
Printed in the United States of America
10 9 8 7 6 5 4 3

*To those visionaries we work with every day
that have the courage and foresight to do the things
that add true value to their organizations*

CONTENTS

Contents

FOREWORD

Computers have been with us now for 50 years. During most of that time they have been used for transaction processing—improving individual applications such as payroll, accounts receivable, inventory management, and order entry. In the past decade, however, this emphasis on isolated applications has been changed in two major ways: There has been a move to "integrated" applications and to an understanding that computer systems need to be based on effective managerial "processes"— linked sets of tasks that allow more efficient processing.

The primary example of integrated applications is the prevalence of enterprise resource planning (ERP) systems. These tie together, in one continuous flow, all the applications that enable the delivery of goods (logistics) as well as related sales and financial applications. Today no major company sets out to implement any major set of applications without ensuring that its underlying managerial approach to the area is well designed.

The authors of this book have carried these two major ideas— application integration based on effective underlying processes—from the transaction area to the world of the organizational management. Effective management starts with strategic planning and moves through many steps to the monitoring and reporting of results. In fact, the authors present eight key processes that must be integrated to provide an effective planning and control environment:

1. Strategy formulation
2. Scenario analysis
3. Planning and budgeting
4. Communication
5. Monitoring
6. Forecasting
7. Reporting
8. Establishing feedback loops

A persuasive case for linking all of these through an integrated system is presented. They note that not only financial data but also nonfinancial performance indicators must be included. Assumptions underlying the development of strategy also must be considered. They term the resulting set of capabilities corporate performance management (CPM).

Recently this integrated approach has received significant attention from software vendors and accounting firms alike. Although many of the underlying ideas have been around for a while, the technology has developed to the extent that this approach is now feasible. In particular, the arrival of relational databases with integrated multidimensional capabilities is a major factor. This book pulls together the underlying ideas and the technical capabilities that allow the effective development of this integrated approach to CPM. The authors also provide interactive Appendices—a Microsoft Word-based series of templates and checklists—that organizations can download and use to implement their own CPM vision. These Appendices can be found at www.wiley.com/go/strategygap (password: Strategy).

We are just at the beginning of managerial use of this integrated set of technically supported managerial processes. Recognizing this, the authors provide not only the rationale behind the approach but also extensive guidance for both getting started in designing appropriate systems and carrying out effective implementation. The 1990s showed the benefits of the integration of transaction processing systems. This may well be the decade of effective integration of the key managerial processes.

> John F. Rockart
> Senior Lecturer Emeritus
> Sloan School of Management,
> Massachusetts Institute of Technology
> Cambridge, MA

PREFACE

That's one small step for man, one giant leap for mankind.

—Neil Armstrong, Astronaut,
Upon setting foot on the moon
July 21, 1969

*We can send people to the moon. Why can't we
implement our strategy?!!*

—Anonymous, CEO,
Upon setting foot in the executive meeting room
July 21, 2002

On a warm autumn day in 1962, a young chief executive stood before a large assembly and introduced a long-term, daring mission for his enterprise. It was both terrifying and inspiring. To many, successfully completing the mission seemed an impossible task.

The executive acknowledged that there was much to do and much to learn before his vision could become a reality. In fact, he probably would no longer be at the helm when the mission was finally completed. He told his audience that taking the actions necessary to achieve the objectives of the mission would require courage—maybe even sacrifice. He knew that not everyone in the organization would understand and support the mission, but he also knew there would be plenty of people willing to help his plan take flight.

He informed his listeners that the competition was well ahead in their quest to be the first to complete the mission. His organization could not afford to allow that to happen. To prevent it, the executive made it clear that top-level support would be given, and the appropriate monetary and other types of resources would be provided to support the planned strategies and tactics. There were many hurdles to overcome and milestones to reach along the road to realizing his vision, but the executive felt confident his people were up to the challenge.

What was that mission? To lead all other nations in the race for space, with the objective of being the first nation to send a man safely to the moon and bring him home again before the end of the decade. Who was that executive? President John F. Kennedy of the United States of America.

Much like Kennedy in the early 1960s, today's CEOs and executives have missions, objectives, goals, strategies, tactics, and key performance indicators for their organizations. But sadly, many organizations fail to fulfill their mission. They create a strategic plan but fail to implement it successfully—if at all.

While organizations understand where they are today and where they would like to be in the future, the road map on how to get there—the strategic plan—seems to remain just a dream. This chasm between the operational plan for today's business and the grand vision for what our business needs to become is what this book calls the "strategy gap."

Businesses have been trying for decades to apply various methodologies and technologies to enhance understanding, decision making, and strategic planning. Why has it not worked? If we can send people safely into outer space and back again, surely there is a way to successfully bridge the gap between the strategic plan and its execution.

If you are an executive who is frustrated with the lack of results generated after the strategic plan has been created, know someone who has no clue that the strategy gap exists in his or her organization but needs to know, or are a young executive interested in making your mark by championing a new idea, much as Kennedy did decades ago, this book is for you.

This book explores how today's systems impact the efficiency and effectiveness of an organization and will help increase readers' understanding of emerging business trends that combine methodologies, systems, and technology to improve corporate performance management (CPM).

This book also provides guidance on selecting the right systems architecture, creating the right team to implement CPM, keys to successfully implementing enterprise-wide CPM solutions, and ideas for calculating the return on investment for CPM applications. Interactive appendices consisting of a Microsoft Word-based series of templates and checklists that organizations can download and use to implement their own CPM vision can be found at www.wiley.com/go/strategygap (password: Strategy).

Today's shareholders demand that organizations execute their strategic plans successfully. We challenge you to use at least some of the ideas in this book to plot your own successful course for eliminating the strategy gap.

ACKNOWLEDGMENTS

Special thanks to our customers for sharing their success stories with us in this book. They continue to inspire us, encourage us, and participate with us as we travel down the corporate performance management road.

Thanks also to our fellow Comshare employees around the world for their continued dedication, spirit of innovation, and can-do attitude.

Finally, thanks to Cindy Morrow and the editors at John Wiley & Sons, Inc. for their valuable contributions in the development and publication of this, our first book.

The Strategy Gap

CHAPTER 1

Strategy Gap

WHAT GAP?

We often come across companies that have set an ambitious long-term goal, perhaps to double revenue and profits over five years, or to dramatically increase the proportion of revenues coming from new businesses, but have devoted almost no intellectual effort to thinking through the medium-term capability-building program that is needed to support that goal. In too many companies there is a grand, and overly vague, long-term goal on one hand . . . and detailed short-term budgets and annual plans on the other hand . . . with nothing in between to link the two together. . . . There seems to be, in many companies, an implicit assumption that the short term and long term abut each other, rather than being dovetailed together. But the long term doesn't start at year five of the current strategic plan. It starts right now![1]

—Gary Hamel and C.K. Prahalad,
Competing for the Future

Long-term goals and detailed, short-term budgets, with nothing to link the two together. Does this organization sound familiar?

Whatever the answer, most business professionals understand that achieving a long-term goal requires a series of logical, achievable, sequential steps. Organizations cannot rely on chance or luck. Yet the steps that lead from where a business is today to where it wants to be—its objectives—often are missing.

1

The "strategy gap," as this group of missing steps is called in this book, is real and exists within most organizations. Often unseen, the gap is a threat to the future performance—and even survival—of an organization and is guaranteed to impact the efficiency and effectiveness of senior executives and their management team.

Imagine for a moment that you are early in your chosen career and the thought of retiring is many, many years away. However, your objective is to retire early, perhaps at 55. To achieve this objective, you have to start planning and executing the plan today. It is no use waiting until you are in your 40s to start executing the plan; it will be too late and you will need to push that retirement date out much farther than desired.

Or consider an oil tanker navigating its way into a port. Newton's law says that a body in motion tends to stay in motion unless something changes it. An oil tanker weighing 500,000 tons requires over an hour and six miles just to slow down from 15 knots. This means that the plan to stop has to be executed well in advance of the intended result.

It is the same in business. Organizations must plan and start executing that plan today if they expect to achieve their objectives some time in the future. Yet surveys indicate that this just is not happening. Despite the increased spending on systems and the technological advances in recent years, only 33 percent of executives take advantage of electronic decision support tools that could help them in managing performance.[2]

The failure of organizations to manage the transition from where they are to where they want to be is one of the most critical management challenges facing senior executives today. Consider that in 2001, more than 250 U.S. organizations—with a combined asset value exceeding $255 billion—failed. As this book is being written, companies are on track to match that figure in 2002. More than 25 percent of the top 100 U.S. companies that survived in 2001 lost at least 66 percent of their market capitalization.[3] Without the ability to achieve objectives, executives and managers become mere bystanders in an organization where performance—or nonperformance—"just happens."

So what is going wrong? What is it about the strategic planning process and its execution that fails? Why do systems so frequently fail to live up to management's expectations? These are crucial questions that need to be answered if the strategy gap is to be avoided.

FAILURE OF STRATEGIC PLANS

According to the dictionary, strategy is "a plan," "an approach," and "a line of attack." There are many different types of strategy, which will be discussed in the next chapter. For now, consider strategy to be "the art of guiding, forming, or carrying out an action plan." When applied to business, strategic planning is about deciding where an organization wants to go and how it is going to get there.

Strategic planning is still the most widely used tool for managing the performance of an organization. In Bain & Company's annual survey of senior executives from around the world, 76 percent of these executives said they look to strategic planning as the top management tool to improve long-term performance and to strengthen integration across an organization. Despite the appearance of many other tools, the report states that senior management trusts familiar tools during difficult times.[4]

Strategic plans typically have a structure that makes them easy to follow. Most start by stating the purpose of the organization, which is usually followed by documenting the long- and short-term goals and the plans for achieving these goals. However, the terminology contained within these plans often varies between organizations, and the words have different meanings. In the context of this book, these definitions will be used:

- *Mission.* A concise statement of the organization's reason for existing
- *Objectives.* Broad statements describing the targeted direction
- *Goals.* Quantifications of objectives for a designated period of time
- *Strategies.* Statements of how objectives will be achieved and the major methods to be used
- *Tactics.* Specific action steps that map out how each strategy will be implemented
- *Key Performance Indicators (KPIs).* Measures of performance that show progress of each tactic in reaching the goals

For its Apollo space program, for example, NASA's strategic plan may have looked something like this:

Mission: Lead all other nations in the race for space.
Objective: Send a man to the moon and bring him back alive.

Goals:	Be the first to do it.
	Do it by the end of the decade.
Strategy 1:	Investigate and select safe landing sites for manned missions.
Tactic 1:	Create and launch a series of unmanned spacecrafts to take and transmit high-quality pictures of the moon back to Earth for scientific study.
KPI 1:	Launch moon reconnaissance spacecraft by the middle of year 2 of the plan and analyze photos by the end of that year.

For a manufacturer of consumer electronics today, the strategic plan may look like this:

Mission:	Be the premier global provider of consumer electronics.
Objective:	Expand the cellular phone product line.
Goals:	Cellular sales for all regions will be 35 percent of total revenue with an overall increase in revenue of 5 percent.
Strategy 1:	Target a new market segment—senior citizens.
Tactic 1a:	Launch a new cell phone with larger pushbuttons and a "panic" button that connects the user immediately with the local emergency response unit, coupled with a special senior citizen discount rate.
KPI 1a:	Produce 1,000 units by May.
Tactic 1b:	Partner with existing national senior citizen organizations for additional user benefits and marketing opportunities.
KPI 1b:	Sign two partnerships by April.

Certainly these examples are simplistic. They are used only to demonstrate the intended meanings of words used in this book. Also for the purposes of this book, it is assumed that organizations know how to prepare a good plan. A typical organization, for example, would have several objectives, each with a set of goals. Each goal could have several strategies, which in turn would have tactics and associated KPIs. Tactics must have measurable KPIs in order to gauge their success. Without these KPIs, an organization has no way of knowing whether a particular strategy worked. Without successful strategies, the organization will not achieve its goals and objectives.

Strategic planning as a management tool has existed for decades. Lack of planning is not causing the strategy gap. According to Hackett Best Practices, a division of Answerthink, companies spend on average nearly five months each year on strategic planning; a little over four months are spent on annual financial planning.[5] This leaves just three months a year when a typical company is not actively planning. A joint report by Cranfield University School of Management and Accenture in-

4

dicates that planning and budgeting consume an astonishing 25,000 person-days annually at a typical $1 billion company. The same report also suggests that 80 percent of companies are dissatisfied with their planning and budgeting processes.[6]

Failure to implement the strategic plan can be disastrous. At best, an organization might achieve acceptable performance based on luck and quick tactical thinking. At worst, the organization may cease to exist. Today's corporate world is littered with the remnants of organizations that failed to implement their strategic plan. An article investigating the reason for the spectacular failure of dot-com companies found that, in most cases, the failures had nothing to do with the strategic plans themselves. The failures resulted from a lack of executing those plans.[7]

So the questions remain: What causes the gap between vision and execution? What can be done to close it? What role should systems play? Based on existing research and experience, the main causes of the strategy gap can be grouped into three areas, each of which interacts with the others:

1. The way management acts to implement strategic initiatives
2. Traditional processes (e.g., budgeting, forecasting, reporting) used to implement strategy
3. Technology systems used to support those processes

MANAGEMENT-INDUCED GAPS

Management can cause a gap between strategy and execution through both action and inaction. Four main ways management causes this gap include failure to secure support for the plan, failure to communicate the strategy, failure to adhere to the plan, and failure to adapt to significant changes.

Failure to Secure Plan Support

The senior management team must develop a strategic plan with objectives, goals, strategies, and tactics that everyone supports. If people do not accept and support the plan, they are unlikely to put in the right amount of effort to make it succeed. Their allocation of resources may be counterproductive to implementing strategic initiatives, while their management time is diverted into seeking out factors that will justify

5

their position. This misplaced time and effort will lead to a gap, which could prevent the execution of the plan.

To achieve buy-in, management must create a corporate culture and a set of values that support the vision and guide employees' decisions and behavior. Employees must have the opportunity to provide feedback regarding their ability to implement strategy. Not listening to their views, not addressing—and resolving—conflicts and major differences of opinion, and not building a learning culture—one that tracks and learns from its own successes, failures, and mistakes—will result in strategies that are unrealistic and cannot be implemented. This situation leads to the strategy gap.

Failure to Communicate the Strategy

Operational managers and their employees are typically the people within an organization who implement strategy. They need to know how the strategy impacts them. Yet according to research by Kaplan and Norton, creators of the Balanced Scorecard, "less than 5 percent of the typical workforce understands their organization's strategy."[8] Without a clear idea of what the strategy, vision, and direction of the organization are, they are unlikely to act in ways that will result in effective implementation of the corporate plan.

Communication of strategy is vital in all management processes. When budgeting, employees need to see the tactical plans and related targets that affect them so they can modify their behavior accordingly. During the year, they need to assess how well they are carrying out those tactics and the progress they are making toward strategic goals. When forecasting, employees need to know when their activities are unlikely to achieve their KPIs and, hence, their strategic goals so they can act early to bring the tactical plan back on target. Technology clearly has a role to play in facilitating this communication. Failure to effectively communicate strategy and how well or poorly it is being implemented will result in the strategy gap.

Failure to Adhere to the Plan

As the year progresses, many organizations make decisions reactively rather than strategically. Often the cause is the reporting of results based on a purely financial view of the organization, such as on the chart of accounts by cost center, rather than by a strategic and tactical view. As a result, operational managers focus on financial variances that do not relate to the specific strategic initiatives outlined in the plan. To put things back on track, the accounts become the target of any decision rather than the agreed-on action plans, which may have long been forgotten.

Test this for yourself. In your current reporting pack, how many of the reports tie actual and forecast results back to the strategies outlined in the strategic plan? The reports may monitor the goals, but how many of them actually monitor KPIs by tactic? Without this link, organizations are likely to act and react in ways that are divorced from the strategic plan, which results in the strategy gap.

Failure to Adapt to Significant Changes

The reality of today's business environment is that it continually changes. Strategic plans are built on a set of assumptions, such as market growth, production capability, and competitor actions. If these assumptions change, it is unlikely that the plan will still hold true. Following the attacks of September 11, 2001, for example, most organizations found themselves in an economy that was substantially different from the one that existed when they planned earlier in the year. Continuing to follow a plan when the basic assumptions on which it was founded have changed makes no sense. Unless plans are modified to reflect changes to these assumptions, the result will be the strategy gap.

PROCESS-INDUCED GAPS

The traditional processes an organization uses to implement and monitor strategy are the second set of strategy gap causes. Once a strategic plan has been researched and created, what happens next? How is the plan translated into action? How are the organization's assets allocated to the various strategic initiatives? How is progress monitored and the success or failure of tactics measured? For most organizations, the key tool used to implement strategy is the annual budget, while the processes of actual reporting and forecasting are used to monitor achievement. But the way in which these processes are approached can lead to the strategy gap.

Lack of Strategic Focus

The objective of any process will determine what gets measured, by whom, and how far in the future. It may seem obvious that the budget should

7

support the implementation of strategy. After all, the purpose of this tool is to control how resources are allocated, which in turn affects what an organization accomplishes. It also may seem obvious that one of the roles of reporting would be to monitor strategic progress. Unfortunately, there is very little evidence to support that these processes actually achieve this. In the report "Driving Value Through Strategic Planning and Budgeting," the authors cite a lack of strategic focus as one of the criticisms of traditional planning and budgeting. Instead of being focused on long-term business health, traditional planning and budgeting are internally driven and focused on current-year profits.[9]

In a survey conducted by Comshare, Incorporated, participants said that there is typically a gap between the strategic plan and the budget created to support it.[10] The budget tends to be financially focused with emphasis on the chart of accounts by cost center, while the strategic plan tends to be behaviorally focused on strategies and tactics. The result is that budget holders, operational managers, and senior executives are often unaware of how strategic initiatives impact the operating plan or whether resources have even been allocated. Without this linkage, the budget becomes a pure numbers exercise, allowing the strategy gap to emerge. As a result, the budgeting and planning processes actually become barriers to strategy deployment.

The same is also true when it comes to reporting actual results and forecasting future performance. For many organizations, reporting of actuals takes the form of a simple income and expense statement by department, based on the chart of accounts. The reason reporting takes this form is mainly because the general ledger holds income and expense items, and these systems are used to generate the reports.

However, strategic plans, which are typically action based and measure activity, do not fit easily within the rigid account and cost center structure of a general ledger, and so the focus is lost. As a result, there is no direction or logical connection in the budgeting and reporting processes for budget holders to adapt their behavior to achieving strategic goals.

Calendar Based

For most organizations, budgeting is an annual process that follows the strategic plan, and it is a process that just takes too long. Hackett Best Practices reports that a typical organization takes over four months to complete a budget cycle.[11] Organizations with an annual budget must try to predict events that are 16 months away, which is unrealistic and leads to the strategy gap. According to Hackett, in today's fast-paced business environment, planning should be treated as a continuous exercise in operational decision making, resource allocation, and performance management. Yet nearly half of organizations treat planning and budgeting as a strictly fiscal and annual exercise that leaves them unprepared to deal with sudden change. Similarly, Hackett found that 74 percent of organizations wait until the end of the month to issue reports.[12] Doing so delays the opportunity to deal with important emerging trends, which could be vital to the effective implementation of strategy. Interestingly, most organizations have the data; it is their processes and tools that let them down. What is required is a planning, budgeting, and reporting process that is triggered by change, not by the date on a calendar.

Financially Focused

An organization's financial results are the outcome of its strategy implementation or lack of strategy implementation. Although some financial measures, such as investments and expenses, will be used in implementing a tactical plan, many of the measures will be nonfinancial. Indeed, the long-term viability of an organization may well rest on the success of nonfinancial measures such as product reliability, customer satisfaction, organizational learning, and the efficiency of the internal processes. The adoption of methodologies like the Balanced Scorecard can ensure that organizations achieve the correct balance of measures that will be needed to achieve corporate objectives. The general ledger by itself will not be able to supply all the data required. As already mentioned, the chart of accounts is a transactional view of an organization. The reliance on this view cannot support the planning and monitoring of strategy and will lead to the strategy gap.

Internally Focused

Consider an organization that sets and achieves a revenue budget that reflects a growth of 10 percent year on year. Is this achievement a good result? Is it a good result if the general ledger confirms that the goal was achieved while staying within the cost budget? What if the goal was built on the assumption that the market was due to grow at 5 percent, when, if fact, it grew at 15 percent? In this case market share was lost rather than gained.

In most organizations today, reports compare the performance of the organization with the budget, not with competitors and the market. Strategy is nearly always based on a combined internal and external view that includes market and competitor assumptions. To ensure that strategy is being implemented, actual reporting needs to compare performance by strategic initiative and to check that any external assumptions made while planning still hold true. Without this strategic external view, decisions will be based on a view of performance that is too narrowly focused, and the strategy gap will develop.

Lack of Realistic Forecasting

Although business conditions can change rapidly, many surprises that affect organizational performance can be predicted using available data and technologies. By predicting future performance from plans based on the current and perceived business environment, contingencies drawn up in advance can be selected or corrections to the existing plan can be made to avoid or exploit the impact of any variances. The ability to recognize and exploit changing business conditions is the driving force behind rolling forecasts—which also deliver the benefit of reducing or eliminating the annual budget process. According to Hackett Best Practices research, however, only 23 percent of organizations make use of this proven best practice.[13]

When forecasting, many organizations once again focus solely on financial results, such as how much revenue will be generated and what the associated costs will be. As with planning, effective forecasting requires modifying and developing plans to achieve strategic goals. In some circumstances, such as when assumptions have changed, strategic goals may have to be reset. Forecasting involves two steps:

1. Predicting the likely future performance based on current knowledge
2. Evaluating or selecting alternative plans to change the predicted outcome

To predict future performance, the natural life cycle of an organization's products and services should be taken into account. This consideration must take place bottom up; that is, each product and service must be analyzed individually. Consider the forecast depicted in Exhibit 1.1.

Exhibit 1.1   According to this forecast, performance
is neither improving nor worsening.

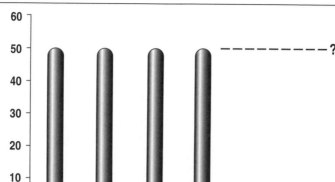

Most people viewing this trend would predict that the forecast would remain level. Now consider the charts in Exhibits 1.2 and 1.3.

Exhibit 1.2 reflects a product that is dying. The forecast suggests that future performance is likely to remain near zero. Exhibit 1.3 represents a product that is growing and whose future performance is likely to reflect a typical life cycle.

Exhibit 1.2   A dying product line.

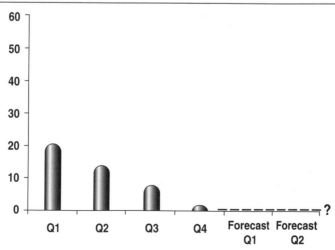

Exhibit 1.3 A growing product line.

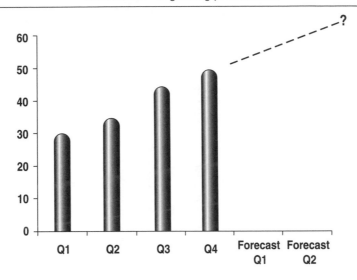

Now consider that Exhibit 1.1 was a summary of the two products shown in Exhibits 1.2 and 1.3. Knowing this, the true forecast is going to be far different from what one might have expected before looking at the individual products (see Exhibit 1.4). Forecasting has to take place from the bottom up to avoid creating misleading results.

Exhibit 1.4 A forecast that considers each product line independently reflects different results from one that summarizes and averages all results.

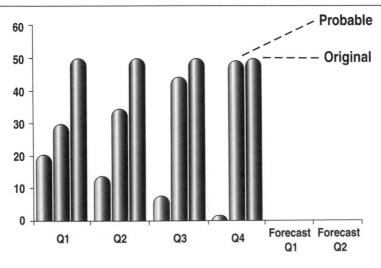

Once a forecast has been generated, it can be used as the basis for "what if" analysis, the process of evaluating alternative scenarios. The aim is to evaluate what changes are required to the tactical plan to achieve the strategic goals. As with budgeting, this evaluation needs to be done by strategic initiative. The result will be the predicted income statement.

Organizations that reduce the forecasting process to a simple extrapolation into the future will reap unrealistic and misleading predictions. They will be unable to modify behavior effectively to achieve strategic goals, which will result in the strategy gap.

Other Factors

Two other factors that can contribute to the strategy gap are more attributable to organizational behavior than to the processes themselves; nevertheless, they need to be taken into account when designing a solution. The first factor is a lack of accountability and commitment to the budgeting process. Budgeting is often a game in which budget holders inflate costs and suppress revenues because they expect senior management to demand reduced costs and increased revenues during a second budget pass. In addition, when a budget is handed down to budget holders without giving them a chance for input, budget holders feel free to miss their targets. After all, it was not their budget. This game playing produces unrealistic budgets, an absence of accountability, and a lack of commitment to the final plan. The result will be the strategy gap.

The second factor is wrongly focused incentive plans. Budget holders and management often are paid on their ability to meet or beat the budget. This fact will affect their decisions when it comes to planning and reporting their performance and does little to help with the implementation of strategy. In some cases it will actively work against the implementation of strategy. Hackett found that when management motivation was linked to strategy rather than to the annual plan, budgeting cycles were reduced and managers were less afraid of taking risks.[14]

TECHNOLOGY SYSTEM-INDUCED GAPS

The third area that causes the strategy gap involves the traditional systems used to support the planning, budgeting, forecasting, and reporting processes. Issues include fragmented systems and misplaced dependence on enterprise resource planning (ERP).

Fragmented Systems

In most organizations, planning, budgeting, forecasting, and reporting are treated as separate, disconnected processes and supported by different technology solutions. In fact, these processes are all part of the much larger process of strategy implementation. The following analogy illustrates why this separation does not make sense.

The journey that a business takes over time is like traveling down a road (see Exhibit 1.5). The road curves and changes direction, and its exact route often is hidden from view. In the same way, business direction continually varies because of changing customer requirements, competitors' actions, or other occurrences in the business environment.

On this journey, the business objective rests on the horizon. This objective, based on current circumstances and assumptions, is the planned destination for the organization. It serves as a beacon, guiding the organization's actions and decisions. The journey is divided into a number of shorter segments, each of which the organization will arrive at over time, allowing the organization to gauge its progress.

To reach the point on the horizon, the traveler outlines a route. This plan identifies the main roads to be traveled and the major cities the traveler will pass through en route to the final destination. In the same way, strategic plans outline the route an organization will travel to reach

Exhibit 1.5 A successful business journey requires knowledge of the starting point, final destination, possible routes, and roadblocks.

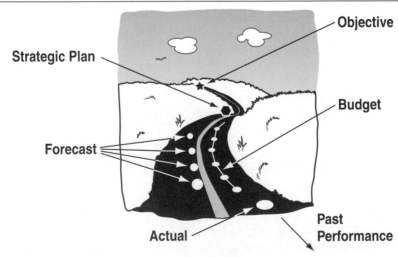

its objective. The journey may take months or years to complete. The key roads are analogous to the strategic plan's tactics that must be performed to achieve the objective. Cities are analogous to key performance indicators that will tell the organization if the tactics have been completed and if it is on target for success.

Continuing, the traveler may plan in greater detail the portions of the journey to be attempted in the near future. The plan may include the names of townships, descriptions of landmarks, and locations of road junctions. These are vital indicators. Without them, the traveler may go in the wrong direction without realizing it until much later. The budget is like that detailed plan outlining the organization's immediate route. It is very much linked to the strategic plan but contains far more detail. With the budget, the business assigns money, people, and assets to the initiatives that will keep the organization on course to reach its objective.

Monitoring progress relative to the detailed plan is a vital activity because it shows the organization whether it is on target. Past performance is of interest, but it actually does little to help the business navigate the road ahead. On the journey, organizations will come up against unexpected diversions, such as construction (activities that are not yet implemented), accidents (activities that are having an adverse impact on performance), and heavy traffic (intense competition for the same customers). These diversions will cause delays and can even lead to dead ends unless the organization can avoid them. Similarly, organizations may come across new roads (new business opportunities) that were not on the map when the journey started. They may discover that taking advantage of these roads can enable them to reach their destination sooner than anticipated.

Finally, like directional signs and mile markers, the forecast tells an organization whether it is heading in the intended direction and where it will end up unless it takes immediate action. The enterprise must monitor position and make adjustments constantly. Occasionally it may need to make a major detour—sometimes even heading in what seems to be the wrong direction—to achieve its final objective. By taking note of the signs—the projected forecasts—and using judgment based on experience, business leaders can make intelligent adjustments to the plan. These adjustments will not be just a once-a-year activity. They may become necessary at any time to keep on track toward the intended destination.

Strategic planning, budgeting, forecasting, and monitoring actuals are all part of the same process—moving an organization toward its objective. Together, they are essential components in the implementation and execution of strategy. When performed in isolation, however, they provide little value.

Quite often, managers are asked to budget using systems that do not allow them to see the strategic plan or latest forecast. It is like asking someone to drive down the road with only partial sight, no map, and no idea of the final destination. To drive performance, the company needs to see the whole travel plan: objective, strategic plan, forecast, actuals, and budget. These elements are all part of the same process.

This journey, or performance management process, is continuous. Markets and competitors do not remain motionless to accommodate an organization's annual planning process. Traveling down this road smoothly and staying on course, like driving a car, requires regular, small adjustments.

Unfortunately, the traditional systems that support planning, budgeting, forecasting, and reporting are inflexible. Each component is isolated from the others. In addition, often each piece of the process is supported by a different technology than the others, causing integration problems. For example, the strategic plan may be presented as a text document; the budget may be prepared in a spreadsheet; actual results may be reported in the general ledger; and analyses may be performed using an online analytical processing (OLAP) tool. These systems are completely disjointed, manually intensive, and error-prone. As a result, they help create the strategy gap. In addition, these systems tend to suffer from other problems that also create gaps:

- *Difficult to change.* Most existing management systems do not allow changes to be made easily. Altering structures, accounts, and basic assumptions so that management can quickly see the impact of change is complex and time consuming. Sadly, most systems are nothing short of glorified adding machines—and they do not even do this very well.
- *Reporting problems.* Systems tend to report from one perspective— usually accounts down the page, and time and version across the page, with each page representing a cost center. Viewing data by product, turnover, geography, or any other business perspective— such as strategy and tactic—is extremely difficult. In addition, many systems require a great deal of effort to disseminate actuals, the latest forecast, and strategy information throughout the organization. These difficulties prevent the detailed analysis of budgets, forecasts, and actual results in context and can result in the approval of unrealistic plans.

16

- *File management issues.* Many organizations still rely on spreadsheets for preparing budgets and reporting results. While spreadsheets are great personal productivity tools, they are a nightmare when used as a corporate planning and reporting system. In addition to flexibility and reporting problems already discussed, spreadsheets and many other file-based systems also incur version control and other problems because multiple files have to be maintained, relinked, and then redistributed. Apart from the time and error-prone nature of this task, you can never be sure that users are now using the right version.

Misplaced Dependence on Enterprise Resource Planning

A second system-induced gap can be caused by the reliance some organizations have placed on their enterprise resource planning (ERP) systems to implement strategy. At first glance, such reliance seems logical.

Before ERP, the processes that made up the supply chain—order entry, inventory management, billing, accounts receivable, and others— were separate functions supported by multiple stand-alone systems, often running on multiple technologies (see Exhibit 1.6). Each part of

Exhibit 1.6 Prior to ERP, the supply chain consisted of multiple processes, technologies, and links.

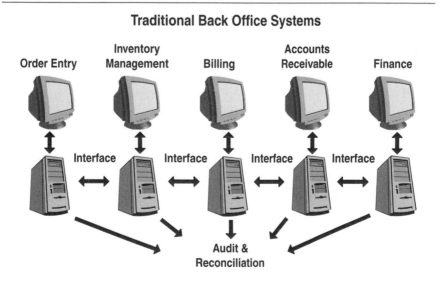

Traditional Back Office Systems

the process could be owned by a different department or operating unit. The problems these systems generated are similar to those encountered with today's planning, budgeting, and reporting systems:

- Expensive in terms of both time (maintenance) and money (hardware and software, personnel). Software had to be maintained on individual desktops. Information technology (IT) staff had to learn multiple technologies. If the system had been created in-house by a person who then left the company, the organization had a big problem.
- Data integrity and version control issues. Changes in one system were not automatically reflected in other systems, data often had to be rekeyed, and data were shared by transferring files. Many departments multiplied by many files equaled trouble. Organizations could never be certain that the information they were basing decisions on was accurate and up to date.
- Organizations could not easily see what was happening across the enterprise, making it difficult to implement corporate strategy, measure its success, and make informed decisions.

Enterprise resource planning was hailed as the solution because it integrated the supply chain processes and supporting systems (see Exhibit 1.7). The ERP systems increased the efficiency and speed of these operations.

Because ERP systems appear to hold most of the actual data in a centralized database, organizations today are looking to these systems to solve their planning, budgeting, and reporting problems. Many organizations are also trying to leverage their huge investments in ERP implementations to get a return. Given that many ERP vendors are now offering "integrated" planning, budgeting, and reporting applications on top of ERP, this initially seems an attractive solution.

The problem, however, is that ERP is the wrong vehicle for implementing strategic plans just as a farm tractor is the wrong vehicle for taking a family on vacation. Gartner, the Stamford, Connecticut–based research firm, reports that "[a]lthough ERP systems have largely addressed the needs of transactional users, they have not been able to address the needs of strategic and operational users."[15] The main reasons given are the complexity of these systems for users and their closed architectures, which make it difficult to integrate non-ERP data. All enterprise resource planning systems are focused on transactions, not on strategy. This very issue is the reason why today's traditional planning, budgeting, forecasting, and reporting systems fail.

Exhibit 1.7 ERP integrated supply chain processes and technologies.

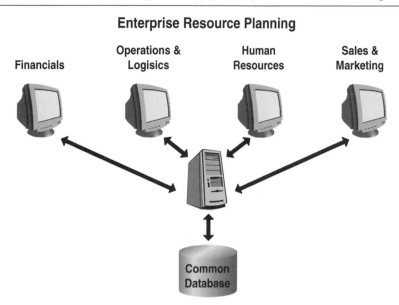

Implementing a strategic plan requires the dissemination of goals, objectives, strategies, and tactics. Planners must be able to evaluate the impact of economic drivers, forecast trends, and predict the impact of competitors. Senior management needs the ability to analyze alternative operating structures, investments, and divestments. Enterprise resource planning was not designed to deliver these capabilities. It is focused on operational efficiency. Implementing strategy is about management effectiveness. The two are different and require different tools and processes.

ROLE OF THE CHIEF FINANCIAL OFFICER

In the past, the role of the chief financial officer (CFO) was to oversee the transactional systems and to report operational performance to investors and management. That role has evolved dramatically in recent years. Today's CFOs are increasingly seen as true business partners in developing and managing the business.

Being a business partner means that CFOs have to increase the value of the finance department by providing leadership in the areas of planning, reporting, and analysis. Today's executives are overwhelmed by the amount of data that technology allows organizations to generate. When this information overflow is combined with dramatically shortened business cycles, increased competitive activity, and a volatile business climate, operations managers and senior executives cannot keep up, are frustrated, and may become ineffective. The finance department, often the custodian of corporate information, must step up to the challenge by providing new business processes and management methodologies and leverage information technology to help enhance organizational effectiveness.

What could be more important and add more value to the business than to help it execute and adjust its plans, avoiding the strategy gap? Chief financial officers and their teams must provide systems and processes that allow organizations to implement strategy. They must provide business methodologies and systems infrastructures to support collaborative strategic planning, budgeting, forecasting, reporting, and analysis that is focused on the execution of strategy. They must provide systems that can disseminate information to those who need it, when they need it, in a form that makes sense to the business user.

Even though IT will enable this environment, Gartner says that IT-driven initiatives in the area of corporate performance management (CPM) will fail.[16] Finance, not IT, must drive any initiative focused on successfully implementing business strategy. Sadly, many finance organizations today are struggling to provide the expected value, particularly when it comes to managing effective budgeting and reporting cycles and giving timely access to results, analyses, and information.

CORPORATE PERFORMANCE MANAGEMENT

Just when executives, buffeted by continually and dramatically changing business conditions, want to throw up their hands and yell, Why bother with planning?, investors and analysts want proof that companies can execute on the promises they make—their mission, objectives, goals, and strategies. In fact, some investors and analysts feel that execution is more important than the strategy itself (see Exhibit 1.8).[17]

It is against this backdrop of execution failure that a new approach to the implementation of strategy is taking shape. "Corporate performance management" is a term coined by Gartner. They describe CPM as "an umbrella term that describes the methodologies, metrics, processes and systems used to monitor and manage the business performance of an enterprise."[18] The concept of CPM has been around for many years but has been identified by many names. For example, Comshare, Incorporated has used the term "management planning and control" (MPC)

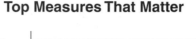

Exhibit 1.8   Investors want proof that corporations can execute strategies.

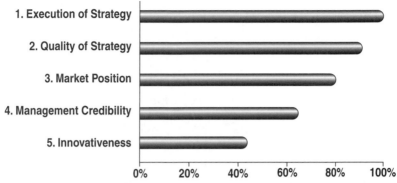

Source: Ernst & Young, Measures That Matter ™

since 1998 to describe the integration of methodologies and processes, while IDC refers to the same concept as "business performance management" (BPM). Whatever term is used, they all refer to the same basic concept of successfully implementing and monitoring strategy.

In the context of CPM, methodologies are the different management techniques and approaches for implementing and monitoring corporate performance. Although many methodologies exist, such as scorecards, activity-based costing, and Stern Stewart's Economic Value Added (EVA), Gartner believes that no single methodology exists for corporate performance management. Organizations will have to blend a number of methodologies together to manage the performance of the enterprise.[19]

Metrics are the specific measures that are used to both manage and monitor the performance of the organization. Some of these metrics will be dictated by the methodology used but will include both financial and nonfinancial measures and will be grouped into both leading and lagging indicators.

Processes are the procedures that an organization follows to implement and monitor corporate performance. Although these can vary widely between organizations, certain key processes are common to all, such as planning, budgeting, forecasting, and reporting.

Systems are the technology solutions that are developed to support the processes that incorporate the chosen methodology(s). They also report on the specific metrics.

All CPM systems leverage technology and best business practices to enable senior executives to confidently and knowledgeably answer questions that help them formulate strategy on an ongoing and real-time basis (see Exhibit 1.9). This is a closed-loop process that starts with understanding where the organization is today, where it wants to go to, what actions have to occur, what goals should be set, and how resources will be allocated to achieve those goals. As plans are implemented, CPM monitors performance of strategies and tactics, highlights exceptions, and provides insight as to why they occurred. From this, CPM systems support the evaluation of alternatives from which decisions can be made—which then leads back to deciding where the organization wants to go.

The technology systems that support CPM must:

- Integrate planning, budgeting, forecasting, consolidation, reporting, analysis, and other processes. A technology system must treat these processes as a continuous course of action, triggered by events rather than by an arbitrary calendar.
- Support methodologies for linking strategy to the allocation of assets (financial and nonfinancial) in support of strategies that can be transformed into action.

Exhibit 1.9   CPM systems help organizations answer questions and formulate strategy.

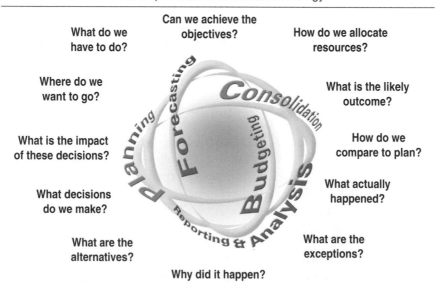

Can we achieve the objectives?

What do we have to do?

How do we allocate resources?

Where do we want to go?

What is the likely outcome?

What is the impact of these decisions?

How do we compare to plan?

What decisions do we make?

What actually happened?

What are the alternatives?

What are the exceptions?

Why did it happen?

- Enable executives to communicate and drive strategy down throughout the entire organization in a way that enables people to act and make decisions that support the strategic goals.
- Focus members of the organization on key issues and critical facts rather than overloading them with data from every aspect of the organization. CPM systems must deliver the right information to the right people at the right time and in the right context.

SUMMARY

In the early days of the race for space, President Kennedy outlined the anticipated rewards of establishing space travel leadership. These included such things as new tools and computers for industry, medicine, and the home as well as new techniques for learning, mapping, and observation. Similarly, business is in the early days of corporate performance management. According to Gartner, there will be rewards for those pioneers who understand and implement CPM first. Gartner predicts, "Enterprises that effectively deploy CPM solutions will outperform their industry peers." They also predict that 40 percent of enterprises will implement a CPM solution by 2005.[20]

Effective CPM will eliminate the strategy gap. The following chapters will explore the design and implementation of effective CPM solutions and how to assess the return on a CPM investment. As Gartner recommends, enterprises should understand the implications of CPM and immediately start building their strategy for deployment.

Where are you on the road to CPM?

Endnotes

1. Gary Hamel and C.K. Prahalad, *Competing for the Future,* Harvard Business School Press, 1994. Reprinted by permission.
2. Hackett Best Practices, a division of Answerthink, Inc., *2002 Book of Numbers: Strategic Decision-Making,* 1.
3. Ram Charan and Jerry Useem, "Why Companies Fail," *Fortune,* May 27, 2002.
4. Darrell K. Rigby, *Management Tools 2001 Global Results* (Boston: Bain & Company, Inc., 2001), 2.
5. Hackett Best Practices, *2002 Book of Numbers,* 8.
6. Accenture and Cranfield University School of Management, "Driving Value Through Strategic Planning and Budgeting" (2001), 4.

7. Diane Franklin, Ph.D., *Mistakes Made by Fast-Growing High Tech CEOs,* www.startupfailures.com/Steps/Step19.htm.
8. Robert S. Kaplan and David P. Norton, *The Strategy-Focused Organization* (Boston: Harvard Business School Press, 2001), 215.
9. Accenture and Cranfield University, "Driving Value Through Strategic Planning," 6.
10. Comshare, Incorporated, "The Comshare 2000 Survey of Top Financial Executives: Planning and Budgeting Today" (2000), 14–16.
11. Hackett Best Practices, *2002 Book of Numbers,* 9.
12. Ibid., 1.
13. Ibid., 3.
14. Ibid., 3.
15. Lee Geishecker and Nigel Rayner, *Corporate Performance Management: BI Collides With ERP,* Research Note SPA-14-9282, Gartner, Inc., December 17, 2001, 3.
16. Nigel Rayner, *Corporate Performance Management Benefits Early Adopters,* Research Note COM-15-9802, Gartner, Inc., May 3, 2002, 3.
17. Ernst and Young, *Measures That Matter™,* 2000, 12.
18. Geishecker and Rayner, *Corporate Performance Management,* 1.
19. Frank Buytendijk and Nigel Rayner, *A Starter's Guide to CPM Methodologies,* Research Note TU-16-2429, Gartner, Inc., May 3, 2002, 1.
20. Geishecker and Rayner, *Corporate Performance Management,* 1.

CHAPTER 2

Strategy in the Next Economy

STRATEGY CHALLENGE

Since the 1960s, the concepts of strategy and strategic planning have engendered a never-ending stream of commentary and debate. No fewer than 20 major business textbooks and thousands of articles are devoted to the topics. Henry Mintzberg, one of the leading authorities on the subjects of strategy and management, has identified 10 major schools of strategic thought.[1] The key question that divides the schools and continues to fuel the debate revolves around the issue of whether it is possible and practical to develop formal strategic plans and implement those plans in the face of an uncertain and unstable environment, such as today's global environment.

Seven of the major schools—the "descriptive" or "emergent" schools—answer the question in the negative. Their basic argument is that the strategy gap cannot be avoided. There is no practical way for an organization to predict and plan for the long term when the future is so uncertain. From this perspective, an organization's strategy and plans are what emerge as the organization attempts to adapt to the changing environment. The other three schools—the "prescriptive" schools—answer the question in the affirmative. This is obviously the position of this book. Formal strategic management (not just strategy or strategic planning) is a necessary requirement for organizational success, especially in turbulent times. From this perspective, the challenge is to develop a strategy that envisions and plans for future uncertainties.

BUSINESS AS UNUSUAL

The 1990s were a time of unprecedented change: the worldwide collapse of communism, the Japanese recession, volatile currency and commodity prices, deregulation, and accelerating technological innovation. Change—reacting to it, anticipating it, and leading it—is always a management challenge. During the latter part of the 1990s, the thriving U.S. economy and booming global financial markets served to mitigate the challenge. This period was labeled the "new economy." As the theory goes, in the new economy the laws of classic economics no longer applied. The balance of activity between firms and the market, between middlemen and the buyers and suppliers they sit between, changed dramatically. The pace of change was too fast for traditional management practices like strategic planning. Instead, managers were encouraged to "outsource to the customer, cannibalize markets, create communities of value, give away information, structure every transaction as a joint venture, treat assets as liabilities, and destroy their value chains."[2] Most important, managers were counseled to "follow the lead of the entrepreneurs and underdogs—seize opportunities in the here and now with a handful of rules and a few key processes."[3]

In the new economy, practical realities were obviously different from theory. As Michael Porter noted in his McKinsey Award–winning *Harvard Business Review* article, "Strategy and the Internet," during this period "both dot-coms and established companies have competed in ways to violate nearly every precept of good strategy," chasing customers indiscriminately, pursuing indirect revenues, offering every conceivable product or service rather than focusing on profits, concentrating on delivering value, and making competitive trade-offs.[4] In March 2000, there were 378 publicly traded Internet companies. Their market cap was $1.5 trillion. Yet their combined annual sales were only $40 billion, and 87 percent never showed a quarterly profit. By the summer of 2001, their market cap had dropped 75 percent, they had laid off 31,000 employees, and 130 had closed their doors. The new economy was over almost before it began.

The rapid demise of the new economy did not lead to a return to business as usual. The factors shaping the new economy—globalization, deregulation, privatization, convergence, disintermediation, and the Internet—continue to mold the competitive landscape. If anything, it is business as "unusual," with the pace of change and discontinuity accelerating. First came September 11, 2001; next Enron and Arthur Andersen; then WorldCom. Unpredictability, uncertainty, volatility, turbulence, and complexity are the order of the day in what has been called the "now" or "next" economy.

Even though the Internet bubble burst, prevailing theory still clings to the belief that traditional management practices, including strategy and strategic planning, have reached their end. The descriptive schools of thought argue that in a complex, chaotic environment, there is no way to plan for the future. A gap between actual results and intended results are the consequence. The descriptive schools assert that formal planning is just a poor way to make strategy. Because the world is unpredictable, strategy will necessarily emerge from attempts to respond to changes in the environment. The more complex and chaotic the environment, the greater the gap between plans and results. Mikela Tarlow puts it this way: "Much of the standard business literature still relies on the idea that we need to define our goals, set priorities, develop our strategies, manage our outcomes and evaluate our impacts. I can assure you that if you operate this way, someone has already beaten you to the finish line. You cannot plan fast enough. We need behaviors that are far more bold and attuned to the unique nature of our time."[5]

Of course, others can just as easily argue that without goals, priorities, plans, or evaluations there is a good chance an organization will not recognize the finish line, much less cross it. In a complex, chaotic environment, the number of potential opportunities can be endless. Without specific goals or objectives, it is difficult to evaluate alternatives. Without specific priorities, there is no way to determine how to allocate resources among the selected alternatives. Without plans, there is no way to guide the actions among those working on the alternatives. Without analysis and evaluation, there is no way to determine which of the opportunities are succeeding or failing.

CHANGE AND UNCERTAINTY

Much of the dialog about the unpredictability of the current environment treats change and uncertainty as if they were binary values—fast or slow, uncertain or certain—and claims that the vast majority of organizations find themselves in the fast and uncertain quadrant. Like any other factors impacting organizational strategy, change and uncertainty need to be thoroughly explored, sliced, diced, and examined.

The new economy is not the first time that companies have been under time pressures. In the early 1980s, the banking industry was completely transformed in three years, following deregulation. Clearly,

27

product cycle times have shortened considerably over the past few years. Yet not all companies are on "Internet time." Cycle times vary considerably from one industry or market sector to the next. For example, pharmaceutical companies, automobile manufacturers, fashion retailers, and financial service firms all have decidedly different cycle times, even though they all operate in today's business environment.

While rapid response may be required to win a battle, it is not necessarily required to win a war. Take, for example, the 11 companies discussed in Jim Collins's book, *Good to Great*. The list includes Abbott, Circuit City, Fannie Mae, Gillette, Kimberly-Clark, Kroger, Nucor, Philip Morris, Pitney Bowes, Walgreens, and Wells Fargo. They share a pattern: "fifteen-year cumulative stock returns at or below the stock market average, punctuated by a transition point, then cumulative returns at least three times the market over the next fifteen years."[6] Taken together, their average return was approximately seven times the market over the 15 years. For these companies, good-to-great did not happen overnight. There was no defining moment, no "killer app," and no sudden miracles. In Collins's words, "the process resembled relentlessly pushing a giant heavy flywheel in one direction, turn upon turn, building momentum until a point of breakthrough, and beyond."[7] Those companies that try to shortcircuit the process are unlikely to succeed.

In the same vein, different organizations and different segments of the same organization face different levels of uncertainty. Uncertainty can come from a variety of sources, both external and internal. In today's world, the overall uncertainty faced by a telecommunications company is clearly greater than the overall uncertainty faced by a large grocery store chain, although before deregulation this was not always the case. Demographic shifts, changes in government regulations, volatility in financial markets, political trends, changes in technology standards, and competitors' moves are all examples of factors that can produce environmental uncertainties.

Hugh Courtney makes a distinction among four levels of uncertainty:

Level 1. *Clear enough future.* The path forward is clear enough to predict the future with a high degree of probability. Companies with stable brands or companies in industries with stable regulations, low rates of technical innovation, and high barriers to entry often face this level of uncertainty. For example, Microsoft probably can predict with a high degree of certainty the near-term demand for its Office products. Similarly, a food manufacturer like Kellogg probably can predict the overall market for a large number of its product lines.

Level 2. *Alternative futures*. The path forward consists of a number of mutually exclusive and exhaustive possibilities, one of which is likely to be chosen or win. This sort of uncertainty is often seen in the world of technology standards. Examples include VHS or Betamax in the world of VCRs, Windows PCs or the Macs in the realm of desktop computers, 2.5G or 3G in the cellular world, and 802.11a versus 802.11b and 802.11g in the wireless world. In each of these cases there was or is no way to predict the eventual winner at the outset, although the alternative possibilities were or are pretty clearly delineated. This sort of uncertainty also arises with pending regulatory and statutory changes. For example, there may be a number of pending legislative alternatives before a regulatory body pertaining to a particular issue (prescription drugs for the elderly, e.g.). There is no way to predict with certainty the outcome of the legislation.

Level 3. *Range of futures*. The path forward consists of a range of alternatives rather than a set of point outcomes. Uncertain product demand is often of this sort. In the future, how much demand by the airlines will there be for "superjumbo" jets? Over the next few years, how many subscribers will sign up for cable Internet connections? While market research and other types of survey information may help provide a range of estimated demand, they cannot pinpoint the specific demand with any accuracy. Unpredictable macroeconomic conditions play a key role in creating this level of uncertainty.

Level 4. *Limited set of future outcomes*. The path forward is unknown and unknowable. The range of possibilities appears limitless. Nascent markets like the early days of e-commerce or the current state of m-commerce (e-commerce via mobile devices) are of this sort. This level also characterizes entry into markets after major political, technological, and social upheavals—such as the changes in Eastern Europe during the 1990s—and markets where the time frames are extremely long—such as projecting demand for renewable energy sources decades out.[8]

From a binary perspective, the world appears to consist of Level 1 and Level 4 uncertainties. From this perspective, there is also a tendency to treat whole industries as if they were one of these two levels. For a given organization, however, uncertainty is issue based, not industry based. For a telecommunications company like AT&T, there is likely greater uncertainty in its broadband and cellular divisions than in its long-distance division. Similarly, most of the strategic decisions faced by managers have Level 2 or Level 3 uncertainties. The potential alternatives or range of alternatives are known. The difficulty is in selecting among the alternatives or narrowing the range in a timely fashion. Over time all situations shift from higher levels of uncertainty to lower levels. The unknown becomes known, potential alternatives surface among the range of possibilities, and winners appear from the range of possibilities. If the organization waits too long, the opportunity may pass it by. If it commits too soon, another alternative may come to the forefront.

With uncertainty, timing is not the only issue that makes strategy formulation and implementation difficult. Other questions also arise: Should the organization simply adapt to the changes over time, or should it attempt proactively to shape the market? Should it focus on a particular alternative, or should it address a portfolio of alternatives? Finally, should the enterprise stick with traditional strategic planning tools and frameworks, or should it adopt a newer framework such as real options, real-time systems, or complex adaptive systems? A book cannot answer these questions. The answers really depend on the specific issues facing each organization and the organization's specific capabilities. However, this book can make the case for sticking with a more traditional system that helps organizations define the strategic issues and determine the level of uncertainty, define the possible alternatives, analyze and select among the alternatives, and monitor and update strategic choices over time.

STRATEGY DEFINED

Given the amount of commentary on the subject, it should be no surprise that the term "strategy" has many definitions. To compound the confusion, the term also is used in combination with a variety of other terms, including corporate strategy, business strategy, functional strategy, strategic thinking, strategic vision, strategic issues, strategic decisions, strategic choices, strategic analysis, strategic planning, and strategic management to name just a few. The common thread running through all the definitions and combinations is the idea that strategy involves a change in the direction and scope of the organization over the long term. It answers the question: Where do we want to go in the future?

A more formal definition describes strategy as the "direction and scope of an organisation over the long-term . . . which achieves advantage for an organisation through its configuration of resources within a changing environment, to meet the needs of markets and to fulfil stakeholder expectations."[9] Based on this definition, a successful strategy delineates a consistent and simple set of long-term goals and objectives based on a thorough understanding of the environment and an objective appraisal of the resources available and needed to accomplish the goals.

A distinction usually is made among corporate, business, and functional strategies. When people speak of the strategies of an organization, they usually are talking about corporate strategies. "Corporate strategies" define the direction and scope in terms of the industries or markets in which the organization plays. Corporate strategies usually involve a top-down, big-picture view of the future. They answer questions such as: Should we diversify our product offerings?; Should we sell or acquire specific businesses?; and What new ventures should we undertake? These strategies usually impact the entire organization, focus on the survival of the organization at a minimum and the creation of substantial added value at a maximum, have a long time horizon (up to several years for strategies involving physical assets), require a substantial commitment of resources, and are not easily reversible.

"Business strategies" are based on a bottom-up, operational view of the organization. They answer questions such as: Should we be a low-cost provider?; What product innovations are needed to capture market share?; and Should we offer different levels of customer support? In essence, business strategies address the issue of how an organization should compete within a particular industry or market. In contrast to corporate strategies, business strategies are operationally specific, are smaller in scope and scale, have a shorter time horizon, and often involve more routine matters.

Finally, "functional strategies" elaborate business strategies. They do this by specifying the direction and scope of the individual functions within a business such as marketing, sales, research and development, finance and accounting, human resources, and others.

When AOL merged with Time Warner in January 2000, it was the culmination of both corporate strategies and business strategies. From a corporate perspective, the acquisition enabled AOL to convert its market capitalization into assets and a revenue stream, supposedly ensuring a cushion against a drop in high-tech valuations. What Time Warner offered was branded content that could be digitized and sold to existing and new AOL subscribers. It also provided AOL access to existing Time Warner cable customers. From a business perspective, the merger solved AOL's bandwidth problems, providing the ability to deliver its service through existing broadband cable connections.[10]

In a multibusiness organization, corporate, business, and functional strategies correspond to the organizational structure (see Exhibit 2.1). Corporate strategies are usually the purview of top management, business strategies are formulated by the individual businesses (divisions or business units), and functional strategies are the responsibility of the functional departments.

Chapter 1 argued that strategic execution, not strategic formulation, is at the heart of strategic failure. Collins's study of the characteristics of "good-to-great" companies lends credence to this argument. In his words: "Strategy per se did not separate the good-to-great companies from the comparison companies. Both sets of companies had well-defined strategies, and there is no evidence that good-to-great companies spent more time on long-range planning than the comparison companies."[11]

In Collins's study, the particular industry played little role in determining success. To be successful, a company did not have to select the right industry. Some of the good-to-great companies were in depressed industries, others in industries with modest growth, and a few were in

Exhibit 2.1   Corporate, business, and functional strategies correspond to the organizational structure.

Types of Strategy by Organizational Level

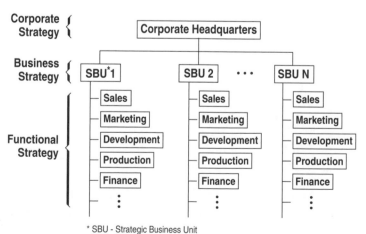

* SBU - Strategic Business Unit

booming industries. This is consistent with other studies that suggest there is little evidence that firms competing in attractive markets necessarily perform better than those in less attractive markets. More important to the transformation from "good-to-great" was focus on a few key drivers and goals and dogged determination (which Collins calls the "hedgehog" concept) in manipulating those drivers to achieve those goals.

STRATEGY MANAGEMENT

Focus is also one of the key variables surfaced in the Hackett Best Practices study mentioned in Chapter 1. Participants in Hackett's studies of key staff functions (finance, strategic decision making, information technology, and related areas) currently comprise nearly 2,000 organizations, including 100 percent of the Dow Jones Industrials, 84 percent of the Dow Jones Global Titans Index, and 90 percent of the Fortune 100. The aim of Hackett's strategic decision-making benchmark study is to determine best practices in the areas of planning and performance measurement. These areas encompass strategic planning, tactical and financial planning, performance measurement, and forecasting. Based on this study, firms that exhibit best practices in these areas are distinguished by four major characteristics:

1. *Integrated.* These organizations employ a well-defined process and methodology for linking strategic plans with tactical plans and goals with measures.
2. *Focused.* They concentrate on a small number of key performance indicators, budget a small number of line items (among world-class firms, 40 or even fewer), forecast only major variables, and report exceptions rather than extensive details.
3. *Fast.* World-class companies exhibiting best practices close their books in 2.9 days and report in one day. World-class, process-focused finance organizations complete their planning and budgeting in fewer than 90 days.
4. *Leverage technology.* They employ a single, integrated system to ensure that they are integrated, fast, and focused, and provide system access to a broad spectrum of users.[12]

Just as the specific industry or market is unimportant in determining success, so are the specific processes and methodologies employed

Exhibit 2.2 Strategic management processes.

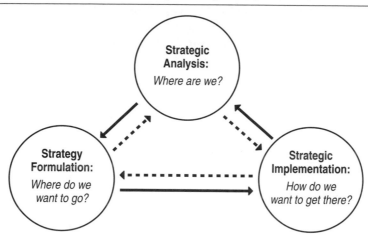

in linking strategies, tactics, and metrics. No one methodology guarantees success. Integration simply requires that systematic actions be taken to formulate and achieve the linkages.

The process of integrating strategies, tactics, and metrics is an essential part of corporate performance management (CPM) and answers these questions:

- Where are we?
- Where do we want to go?
- How do we want to get there?

Strategic analysis, strategy formulation, and strategy implementation are the processes used to address these questions. Exhibit 2.2 diagrams the interrelationships among these processes. Each of these processes encompasses a number of subprocesses that will be covered in detail in Chapter 3.

INTEGRATING TOP-DOWN AND BOTTOM-UP STRATEGIC MANAGEMENT

In many organizations there is a tendency to equate strategy with corporate strategy and to define it even more narrowly in terms of strategic development. In these organizations, top-level management is focused on the question: Where do we want to go? Their emphasis is on understanding the competitive environment and creating a vision for the future. The more mundane question of How do we plan to get there? is ignored. Once the annual planning meetings are held and the strategic plan is produced, the plan is either put on the shelf or tossed over the fence to operations. If things go astray, the top level will pressure the operational level to try harder.

The view from the other side is often the opposite. Many lower-level managers state that the key to organizational success is operations—the efficiency with which the day-to-day grind of production, selling, marketing, servicing, and the like are performed. If things go astray, these same managers will also tell you that senior management just does not understand the operational challenges and the decisions they face on a daily basis and the inherent need for fast action in the face of competitive challenges.

Clearly, operations are an important element in the strategic landscape. However, there is a difference between action and execution. Operations need to be tied with strategic objectives. As Gerry Johnson and others put it: "[I]f the operational aspects of the organization are not in line with the strategy, then, no matter how well considered the strategy is, it will not succeed. . . . It is at the operational level that real strategic advantage can be achieved."[13]

For instance, consider what happened to the United Kingdom's retail firm Laura Ashley. The firm started as a husband-and-wife (Laura and Bernard Ashley) operation producing scarves in their flat in London. During the 1980s they became a globally successful fashion and retail firm providing a product line of clothing, accessories, and home furnishings with a unique look and appeal. After the death of the firm's namesake in the mid-1980s, top management seemed to lose direction. During the 1990s regional managers were allowed to institute operational systems based on the specific demands in their regions. The regional stores also tried to service the immediate needs of their customers. There was no overall vision for the hundreds of Laura Ashley stores located across the world. The firm's performance suffered accordingly. Only recently has it started to make a comeback after several years of recurring losses. The fate of Laura Ashley is typical of firms whose managers "simply respond to what happens around them . . . with no anticipation of what might happen and no hope of shaping what could happen."[14]

Successful CPM requires not only horizontal alignment of the individual processes—analysis, direction, and implementation—but also vertical

Exhibit 2.3 Top-down and bottom-up inputs and outputs for strategic management processes.

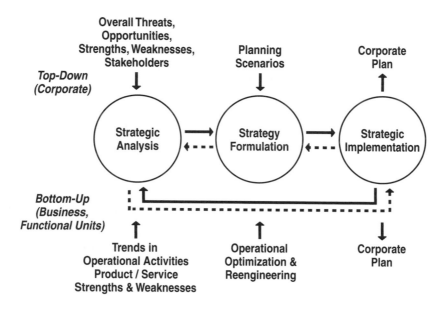

Aligning Top-Down and Bottom-Up Views

alignment of the top-down and bottom-up views of the organization. These views need to be reconciled, synthesized, and coordinated across each of the CPM processes. Exhibit 2.3 summarizes the required inputs and outputs from and to the top and the bottom for each of these processes.

During strategic analysis, information and knowledge has to come from both the top and the bottom. The top-down perspective offers a consolidated picture of the overall environmental threats and opportunities facing the organization, the combined strengths and weaknesses of the resources within the individual operational units, and the collective expectations of all the stakeholders inside and outside the organization. The bottom-up perspective provides a series of individual images highlighting the trends in various operational activities and the relative strengths and weaknesses of specific products and services in comparison with those of specific competitors.

From the standpoint of strategy formulation, the consolidated top-down analysis can be used, for example, to create various planning scenarios. These planning scenarios can help define or redefine the organization's future directions, its strategic choices, and its overall port-folio of products and services. The bottom-up analysis can help identify potential innovations in products and services and possible areas for op-erational optimization and reengineering. The bottom-up analysis also can serve as the basis for various planning models. Taken together, these can help answer questions about the potential outcomes of various strategic options for the individual operational or business units making up the organization.

Finally, the process of strategic implementation will result in a se-ries of plans and programs for both the top-down organizational level and the bottom-up operational level. The number of plans and pro-grams will depend on the number of products, industries, and markets served by the organization. As Exhibit 2.4 indicates, the number of im-plementation plans and programs obviously increases as the combina-tion of products, industries, and markets increases. Fortunately, recent CPM systems enable an organization to provide a single online source for accessing, monitoring, and controlling the combined top-down and bottom-up strategies, objectives, tactics, and key performance indica-tors (KPIs) regardless of the number of products, industries, or markets involved.

DISCONTINUITIES

Strategy formulation requires management to predict the future. Based on these predictions, management makes strategic choices about com-pany direction, focus, and resource allocation. By their very nature, strategic choices impact the entire organization, have long time hori-zons, require a substantial commitment of time and money, are not eas-ily reversed, and can impact the organization's survival.

In today's business world, the level of uncertainty makes the future hard to predict. Uncertainty, however, is not the only reason it is diffi-cult. The business world is an example of a complex system. Complex systems are hard to predict because they exhibit "punctuated equilib-rium." These systems are characterized by long periods of stability in which continuous, incremental changes occur that are disrupted by dra-matic, discontinuous change. This pattern of stability interspersed with discontinuous change is called punctuated equilibrium.[15] Punctuated equilibrium makes it difficult to craft a strategy that can handle incre-mental improvements in existing products and services while simulta-neously trying to introduce new products and services. "Strategic vision

Exhibit 2.4 The number of plans and strategies increases as the combination of products, industries, and markets increases.

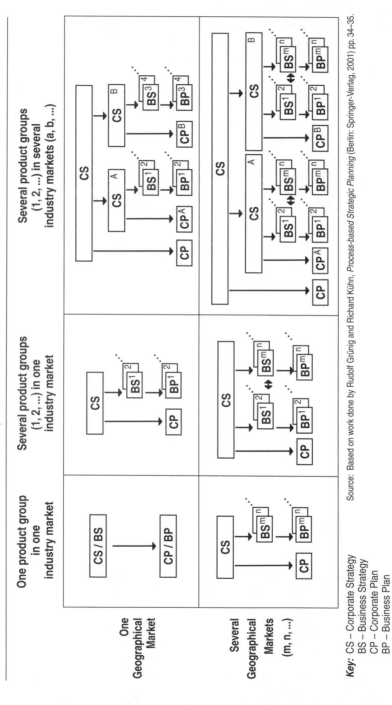

Source: Based on work done by Rudolf Grünig and Richard Kühn, *Process-based Strategic Planning* (Berlin: Springer-Verlag, 2001) pp. 34–35.

Key: CS – Corporate Strategy
BS – Business Strategy
CP – Corporate Plan
BP – Business Plan

that foresees discontinuities and strategic planning that prepares for discontinuities are the key challenges to strategic thinking."[16]

The changes that have occurred in the NASA space program over the years provide a hint of how organizations can develop and implement strategies in the face of punctuated equilibrium. We have already recounted the Apollo program—America's race to be the first country to put a man on the moon. America succeeded in putting men on the moon—six missions in all. The first success was *Apollo 11* (July 1969). The last success was *Apollo 17* (December 1972). The Apollo program had all the trappings of a "big" strategic decision. It was a long-term decision. It was very risky. It cost a lot in time, money, and people. Additionally, there was never any intention to reverse the decision. Thirty years later, the space program bears little resemblance to the earlier days. With programs like the Lunar Prospector and Mars Sojourner, NASA has moved from a "big-ticket" approach to a new "smaller, faster, cheaper" approach. The Lunar Prospector, for instance, cost $63 million to build and launch. This compares with the $266 million for an Apollo launch. Even if it fails, NASA still has money for four more tries. Basically, with programs like the Lunar Prospector, NASA has moved into an era of experimentation with smaller, cheaper probes.

Experimentation is one way to handle both uncertainty and discontinuity. Hugh Courtney describes three distinct approaches to handling uncertainty and discontinuous change:

1. *Contingent road map.* A contingent road map lays out the changes that might occur in an organization's future and possible adjustments that an organization can make in response to those changes. A contingent road map focuses on key uncertainties, describes the exhaustive set of possible future outcomes, identifies key trigger events for each contingency, and delineates the strategic actions for each contingency. Contingency road maps are continuously revised, based on analysis. They not only recommend strategic changes but also help create those changes.

2. *Option portfolio management principles.* In the volatile worlds of energy, gas, oil, and futures trading, financial brokers use a portfolio of options to hedge their trades. The options are used to minimize their investments. An option is a right, but not an obligation, to buy an asset within a certain time. If investors' predictions are right, then they will execute the trade. If not, they will let the option expire, forfeiting the option fee but not the entire value of the original trade. Special mathematical

techniques—such as the Black-Scholes method—are used to value these options. Those brokers who utilize options to trade in these markets know they will not win every time. Their goal is simply to win many more times than they lose. The application of options theory to strategic development is straightforward. In uncertain environments, it is better to place low-cost bets on a variety of outcomes—that is, the strategy portfolio. Each strategy in the portfolio is broken down into a smaller set of sequential objectives. As time passes, decisions are made about whether to continue the investment in the strategy or to pull the plug. Doing this avoids placing big bets on uncertain outcomes that jeopardize the future viability of the organization.

3. *Strategic evolution.* In those situations with the highest levels of uncertainty (Level 4 uncertainty discussed earlier), there is a need to quickly identify new threats and opportunities and to make quick decisions and aggressive commitments. This can be accomplished through a number of practices including scanning (using early warning systems to detect changes), experimenting (developing smaller experimental programs to learn more about existing threats and opportunities), monitoring (providing real-time access to experimental results), and committing (using the information to make go/no-go decisions about experimental projects).[17]

SUMMARY

In 1998 Larry Downes and Chunka Mui published a book called *Unleashing the Killer App.* They defined a "killer app" as "a new good or service that establishes an entirely new category and, by being first, dominates it, returning several hundred percent on the initial investment."[18] Killer apps destroy and re-create industries far from their immediate use and throw into disarray the complex relationships among business partners, competitors, customers, and regulators of markets.

In an obvious reference to Downes and Mui's work, Willie Pietersen introduced the notion of "killer competencies."[19] Killer competencies are those few things that an organization must do well to have a winning strategy in today's uncertain environment. These killer competencies are very similar to the characteristics of best-practice firms identified by Hackett Best Practices. The list of competencies also summarizes many of the main points made in this chapter. The five killer competencies include:

1. *Insight.* Superior ability to make sense of the changing environment is critical.
2. *Focus.* While any number of implementation plans and programs can be undertaken, a key to success is single-minded dedication to one strategic vision.
3. *Alignment.* Organizations need to align every element—structures, processes, skills, measurements, rewards, and culture—with the organization's focus.
4. *Execution.* Successful organizations develop the ability to implement a strategy quickly, expanding the gap between the organization and its competitors and improving the organization's response to the next set of changes.
5. *Renewal.* Organizations must create an ongoing cycle of learning, focusing, aligning, and winning.

With this more complete understanding of strategy for the next economy in hand, it is time to look at CPM processes—the mechanism by which organizations close the strategy gap.

Endnotes

1. Henry Mintzberg and Joseph Lampel, "Reflecting on the Strategy Process," in Michael Cusumano and Constantinos Markides, eds., *Strategic Thinking for the Next Economy* (San Francisco: Jossey-Bass, 2001), 33–54.
2. Larry Downes and Chunka Mui, *Unleashing the Killer App* (Boston: Harvard Business School Press, 1998), 77.
3. Kathleen M. Eisenhardt and Donald N. Sull, "Strategy as Simple Rules," in *Harvard Business Review on Advances in Strategy* (Boston: Harvard Business School Press, 2002), 115–116.
4. Michael E. Porter, "Strategy and the Internet," in *Harvard Business Review on Advances in Strategy*, (Boston: Harvard Business School Press, 2002), 1.
5. Mikela Tarlow with Philip Tarlow, *Digital Aboriginal* (New York: Warner Books, 2002), xvi.
6. Jim Collins, *Good to Great* (New York: HarperCollins, 2001), 6.
7. Ibid., 14.

8. Hugh Courtney, *20/20 Foresight* (Boston: Harvard Business School Press, 2001), 28–34.
9. Gerry Johnson and Kevan Scholes, *Exploring Corporate Strategy,* 5th ed. (London: Prentice-Hall Europe, 1999), 10.
10. Frederick Betz, *Executive Strategy* (New York: John Wiley & Sons, 2001), 11–12.
11. Collins, *Good to Great,* 10.
12. Hackett Best Practices, *2002 Book of Numbers: Strategic Decision-Making* (2002).
13. Johnson and Scholes, *Exploring Corporate Strategy,* 10.
14. Shona L. Brown and Kathleen M. Eisenhardt, *Competing on the Edge* (Boston: Harvard Business School Press, 1998), 141–142.
15. Willie Pietersen, *Reinventing Strategy* (New York: John Wiley & Sons, 2002), 30.
16. Betz, *Executive Strategy,* 31.
17. Courtney, *20/20 Foresight,* 136–150.
18. Larry Downes and Chunka Mui, *Unleashing the Killer App* (Boston: Harvard Business School Press, 1998), 4.
19. Pietersen, *Reinventing Strategy,* 53–56.

CHAPTER 3

Corporate Performance Management Processes

EVENT-DRIVEN APPROACH

Processes are the mechanism by which organizations implement and monitor strategy. Gartner refers to them as the "glue" of a corporate performance management (CPM) system, binding together the management methodologies and metrics in a way that allows the development, communication, funding, and measurement of strategic initiatives.[1]

Today the CPM processes of planning, budgeting, forecasting, and reporting are typically calendar driven. But this method comes from a historical perspective, when the pace of business was slow enough to allow a monthly reporting cycle and an annual budgeting process to be sufficient for most needs. In today's fast-paced business environment, organizations do not have the luxury of time. Waiting for the month end to see an initiative's result could cause delays in correcting performance and result in unnecessary cost. Similarly, waiting for an annual budget process to implement a strategic change could be fatal.

Events drive CPM processes. For example, if an assumption used to create the plan or budget changes dramatically or a key performance indicator (KPI) shows that the organization is not going to meet its strategic goals, the appropriate CPM processes are invoked immediately. There is no need to wait until the next scheduled planning or budgeting cycle to make the change.

Achieving organizational objectives requires constant monitoring of signs (actual and forecast) and responding to exceptions. Any KPI that falls outside of expected values or differs from basic assumptions triggers the appropriate process or processes to put the company back on track. This triggering is achieved through feedback loops within and between each CPM process. When a process is activated, only the affected areas are replanned. For example, if the core business is operating successfully but a new initiative is in trouble, there is no reason to replan the core business. Replanning the initiative may be sufficient to achieve corporate goals. For this reason, operational groups and their contribution to strategies and associated tactics should be identified and planned as discrete sets of resources wherever possible.

KEY CPM PROCESSES

Although the amount and type of processes may vary, a number of key processes are common across most organizations and industries. These processes relate to strategy management as defined in Chapter 2. Exhibit 3.1 provides an overview of these key processes as defined by Gartner.[2] In this case, the report process encompasses strategic analysis, the strategic formulation and scenario analysis processes equate to strategic development, and the remaining processes combine to form strategic implementation.

Processes define the way in which users from all parts of the organization interact with each other in implementing organizational strategy. Three types of users are involved in CPM processes:

1. Executives responsible for the formulation of strategy and associated goals
2. Operational managers responsible for defining and executing tactical plans to achieve corporate goals
3. Transactional users—the employees who carry out the day-to-day activities of the organization

In Exhibit 3.1, the bold lines illustrate how each process feeds the next logical process to ensure that strategies are communicated, implemented, and monitored. The faint and dotted lines represent feedback loops that trigger an alternative process based on an event and provide for adjustments to strategy and/or tactics if results differ from those

Exhibit 3.1 Common CPM processes and feedback loops.

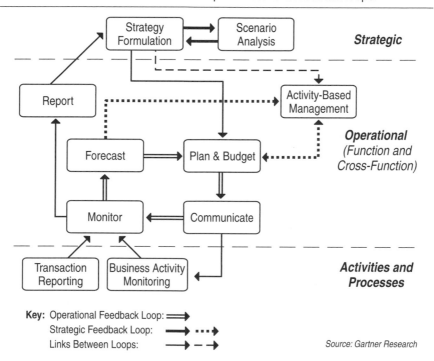

planned. Without feedback loops, each process becomes isolated and prevents continuous performance management. Each CPM process encompasses a number of subprocesses, many of which can be performed with the aid of various tools and methodologies. Exhibit 3.2 summarizes the major subprocesses with some of the associated tools and methodologies that can be used. Activity-based management (ABM) can be thought of either as a separate process that monitors the cost or contribution of an organization's activities or as a methodology in which activity becomes the building blocks of a plan.

Processes have these characteristics:

- Each process has an input that is supplied from a previous process or from one that triggered it. Each process has an output that either feeds the next logical process or triggers a feedback loop to another one. Exhibit 3.3 shows the input and output of each process.

Exhibit 3.2 Major CPM subprocesses and associated tools.

CPM Process Name	Sub-Processes	Tools or Techniques
Strategy Formulation	Environmental analysis	
	Resource and capability analysis	Benchmarking
		Portfolio analysis
	Stakeholder analysis	Stakeholder mapping
	Scenario generation	Product/market matrix
		Profit zones
Scenario Analysis	Scenario evaluation	Strengths, weaknesses, opportunities, threats (SWOT)
	Scenario selection	Life cycle analysis
		Portfolio analysis
		Value chain analysis
		Ranking
		Decision trees
		Scenario planning
		Profitability analysis
		Cost-benefit analysis
		Shareholder value analysis
		Financial ratio analysis
		Sensitivity analysis
		Simulation
		Funds flow analysis
		Break-even analysis
		Resource deployment analysis
Plan & Budget	Tactical plan: development of tactics and KPIs in line with strategies and goals	Balanced Scorecard
		Economic Value Add (EVA)
		Activity-based management
	Resource allocation: assigning resources to tactical plans	Revenue planning
		Production planning
		Salary planning
		Capital planning
		Threshold planning
	Budget review	
	Threshold planning	

CPM Process Name	Sub-Processes	Tools or Techniques
Communicate	Changing organizational behavior to implement tactics	Web portals
		Team meetings
		Kick-off conferences
Monitor	Review financial plan	Balanced Scorecard
	Review tactical plan	Alerts
	Review assumptions	
	Transaction reporting	
	Business activity monitoring	
Forecast	Statistical extrapolation	Time series analysis
	Forecast collection	Simulation
	Forecast review	Sensitivity analysis
	Scenario evaluation	Exchange exposure analysis
	Communication	
Report	Production and distribution of management accounts	
	Adjustment and audit for financial consolidation	
	Analysis of results	

- Each process operates as a closed loop, that is, processes are cyclical within themselves (the budget process may undergo several iterations—or cycles—before it is complete, as may the forecast and report processes) and as a whole.
- Processes take place at different times and at different frequencies, and may involve different people depending on the result of a feedback loop.

The key CPM processes must be integrated, which means more than just providing a simple linkage. Daniel Gray found that only by developing systems that implement all the processes as a consistent whole could business strategies be executed well.[3] Each of these processes is now considered in more detail.

Exhibit 3.3 Inputs and outputs of major CPM processes.

CPM Process	Input to Process	Output from Process
Strategy Formulation	Organization mission and objectives External research Analyses from report process	Organizational objectives Strategies and associated goals Assumptions
Scenario Analysis	Various strategic scenarios	SWOT analysis Summary financial plan
Plan and Budget: Tactical Plans	Strategies and associated goals Assumptions SWOT analysis Summary financial plan Forecast	Tactics and associated KPIs Top-down targets
Resource Allocation	Summary strategic plan Tactics and associated KPIs Top-down targets	Resource allocation Financial plan (budget) Capital plan Cash flow forecast Threshold levels
Communicate	Resource allocation Strategies and tactics	Action plan
Monitor	Actual results External assumption update Transaction exception alerts Tactical plan review	Updated scorecard with exceptions highlighted
Forecast	Actual results	Statistical projection exceptions from budget Adjustments to tactical plan
Report	Actual and forecast results	Management accounts Financial consolidated accounts Analyses

Strategy Formulation

Most strategic planning cycles begin with some kind of situation analysis. This analysis is designed to determine the key external and internal factors that currently influence or will likely influence the overall direction of the organization. Situation analysis is really an umbrella term covering a number of different types of analyses including:

- *Environmental analysis.* This is sometimes called PEST analysis. It identifies the major *p*olitical, *e*conomic, *s*ocial, and *t*echnological influences coming from outside the organization and their potential impact on the organization's near-term and long-term direction.[4]
- *Resource and capability analysis.* An organization fulfills its short- and long-term vision and objectives by deploying its tangible assets (financial and physical resources) and intangible assets (intellectual property, brands, employee skills and knowledge, etc.). This type of analysis not only determines which of those assets are key to the organization's strategy, it also determines the organization's capacity to employ these assets for accomplishing particular productive activities. Benchmarking and portfolio analysis are two techniques used to assess the viability of these assets and their relative position with respect to competitors.
- *Stakeholder analysis.* Value created by the firm is distributed among a variety of parties (e.g., investors, employees, suppliers, partners, etc.). Each of these stakeholders has different expectations that can impact the scope and direction of the organization. This form of analysis provides an understanding of the various expectations. Stakeholder mapping can be used to establish the interest and power of key stakeholders.[5]

The output of this process are organizational objectives and goals to be achieved in the short and medium term.

Once the situation analysis is complete, the next step is to specify the options available for achieving those goals and objectives, delineate the criteria for evaluating those options, and employ the criteria to select those options the organization will pursue. In a general sense, all strategies either revolve around the preservation of existing opportunities or the development of new opportunities. A traditional product/market matrix (see Exhibit 3.4) provides a broad outline of

Exhibit 3.4 Traditional product/market matrix.

Products and Services

Markets	Existing	New
Existing	**Protect/Build** • Withdrawal • Consolidation • Market Penetration	**Product Development** • On existing competencies • With new competencies
New	**Market Development** • New segments • New territories • New uses	**Diversification** • On existing competencies • On new competencies

Source: From *Exploring Corporate Strategy,* Gerry Johnson and Kevan Scholes. © Prentice Hall Europe 1984, 1988, 1993, 1999, reprinted by permission of Pearson Education Limited.

some of the potential options available to an organization for determining forward direction.

In the same vein, Adrian Slywotzsky, David Morrison, and others have delineated 22 models/patterns of profitability that explain how profits are generated in various businesses. Some examples include "customer solutions profit," "product pyramid profit," and "multi-component system profit."[6] In contrast to classic productcentric models that focus on market share, increased volume, and economies of scale, these profit models answer the questions: Where can we make profit in our industry? and How should I design my business to be profitable? Another way for managers to understand potential directions and strategic options is by understanding the various models.

The different options are evaluated in the scenario analysis process where they can be selected singly and in combination to go forward to the plan and budget process. Having a portfolio of such options means that alternatives can be substituted should any selected scenario fail to achieve expectations.

The output from this process will be a strategic plan that specifies in detail the organization's forward direction (the mission, vision, and values), higher-level goals, objectives, and strategies. It will also incorporate the strategic analysis on which its forward direction is based. Goals will be supported by a summary financial plan that shows how resources will be deployed and identifies the assumptions about the internal and external business conditions that were made.

Scenario Analysis

This process works in conjunction with the strategy formulation process. It encompasses the evaluation and selection of suitable options for the strategic plan. The evaluation process usually involves a sequence of four steps:

1. The suitability of each option is weighed. Suitability addresses the simple question of Why is this a good idea in the overall context of the organization? Some of the techniques for assessing suitability include life-cycle analysis, portfolio analysis, and value chain analysis.
2. The relative merits of the suitable options are compared using techniques such as ranking, decision trees, and scenario planning.
3. The acceptability or expected performance and risk of each of the highly ranked options are determined next. Expected performance can be determined by using various numerical tests, such as profitability analysis, cost-benefit analysis, and shareholder value analysis. Risk can be assessed using financial ratio analysis, sensitivity analysis, and simulation modeling.
4. The final question to be addressed is whether the organization has the resources to implement an option. Funds flow analysis, break-even analysis, and resource deployment analysis can be used to gauge this.

Once the options have been evaluated, the selection process can begin. The basic purpose of any strategy is to add value and contribute to the competitive position of the organization over the long term. While no algorithm can be used to determine the contributions of a particular strategy, some general criteria can be employed. These include:

- Consistency with mission and objectives
- Suitability (as determined by techniques such as SWOT [strengths, weaknesses, opportunities, and threats] analysis)
- Validity of the assumptions and information underlying the strategy
- Feasibility with respect to resources, commitment, and competitive reaction
- Risk and the acceptability of the risk
- Attractiveness to stakeholders.

51

Plan and Budget

Tactical Plan. The success of a strategy lies in its implementation. General George Patton once said that people should not be told *how* to do something; rather, if they are told *what* to do, they will act with surprising ingenuity. Once operational managers know and understand the *what*—the organizational strategies and goals—they will be able to come up with the *how*—the detailed tactical plans. The plan and budget process is where detailed operational plans are created to implement the strategies that deliver the goals defined in the strategy formulation process. These plans are supported during the budgeting process by the allocation of the appropriate resources.

Tactical plans can be developed from a number of different organizational perspectives. Many large organizations plan by strategic business unit or product. Some organizations, such as defense contractors and oil exploration companies, tend to develop plans by project. In these cases, the different functions within the organization plan their role in delivering the contract or project.

An operational plan is more like a project plan. It delineates the organization's short-term tactics, measures, tasks, responsibilities, deadlines, and initiatives. The KPIs within the plan can show both that tactics are being implemented and that they are achieving the desired results. With newer strategic planning methodologies and systems (see Chapter 4), there is no real distinction between the strategic plan and the operational plan. Instead, the strategic plan is an online representation that succinctly documents the key planning objects (both strategic and operational) and the linkages among them. For example, a balanced scorecard system provides online access to an organization's mission and vision along with its major strategic objectives, measures, targets, and initiatives. In this sort of system, the plan becomes an active document that provides a real-time view of where the organization stands with respect to its strategic objectives.

Some organizations group the plan's activities into two categories. The first category is concerned with continuing operations, while the second deals with new strategic initiatives. Brisbane City Council, for example, took this latter approach and planned continuing operations at a summary level because income and expenses were pretty well known. This saved the council members time and allowed them to concentrate on the detailed planning of new projects. This level of detail ensured that each initiative was properly funded and allowed council members to rank and select initiatives should budget pressure cause them to reduce expenditure.

What is important about this process is the way operational management works with executive management to develop measurable action plans. Executive management understands what needs to be achieved, while operational management has the experience and knowledge to know what can be achieved given the assumptions being made. In addition, operational management has a stake in making sure that tactics and associated KPIs are realistic because they are the ones who will be held accountable for implementation.

Resource Allocation. Resources are scarce. If they were not, organizations could simply throw people and money at all their problems and would overwhelm the competition. Because of this scarcity, organizations must put their money and their people where their strategies are. An organization's strategic objectives and key metrics should serve as top-down drivers for the allocation of an organization's tangible and intangible assets. While continuing operations clearly need support, key resources should be assigned to the most important strategic programs and priorities. Most organizations use their budgets and compensation programs to allocate resources. By implication, both of these need to be aligned carefully with the organization's strategic objectives and tactics to achieve strategic success.

The best way to achieve this alignment is to allocate and budget resources to the tactical plans. The perspective(s) chosen for entering the budget should reflect the perspective used in the tactical plan. For example, if one of the tactics is to develop a new sales channel, then the cost of setting up that channel and revenues from that channel by product need to be planned at that level. Without this, there would be no way of measuring the success of those tactics and, hence, the strategy. This linkage helps organizations avoid, for example, the problem of random budget cutting that affects associated strategies. Budgeting by tactic helps to identify the potential impact on strategy implementation.

The budget process has a logical structure that typically starts with tactics that generate some form of income, whether from subscription or from sales. In organizations that sell goods or services, this logical structure is based on their ability to produce or to obtain the right amount of goods and services to sell. Once an income figure has been established, the associated costs of delivering that level of income can be generated. Quite often this will entail input from other departments or tactics. These users will need information such as price, volume, and other drivers before they can start on their own plans. This means the process has to be collaborative and that dependencies between functions need to be clearly communicated and understood. Additionally, the various overheads of the organization and the capital that will be required must be determined. This information, once consolidated, will show the cost by tactic as well as the cash and funding requirements to put the plan into operation.

To aid the budgeting process, budget holders will need information on each tactic and an idea of the target to be achieved. That is the role of the top-down target generated at the end of the tactical plan sub-process. This target guides the budget holders in terms of what they should try to achieve. If they believe they can better the target or feel that the target is unattainable, the process needs to capture their feedback and deliver it to operational management.

Budget Review. Once a budget has been collected, a thorough review needs to take place to ensure that the plan is realistic, implementable, and meets strategic goals. Doing this requires a review methodology that answers these questions:

- Which tactics have KPIs that are outside of the top-down goals? If budget holders cannot meet the top-down targets, then the affected strategic goals may not be achievable. Budget holders should provide an explanation for any values outside of targets.
- Which major income or cost items show an abnormal trend compared with last year? Game playing (budget holders holding back revenues or inflating costs) produces unrealistic budgets. Charting the seasonality of the current planned budget versus last year's budget sometimes can identify this occurrence. Similarly, using statistical techniques to extrapolate metrics and compare them with the budget can give an indication of potential discrepancies.
- What major income and cost items show an abnormal increase or decrease between the planned budget and the actual budget? If the start of the budget period shows an unrealistic step up or step down from the end of the current actual or forecast period, as illustrated in Exhibit 3.5, the budget may be unrealistic. Any significant step needs an accompanying explanation.
- How far are budget tactics from top-down targets? Produce a list of tactics sorted by budget variance from top-down targets. This list enables management to focus on those tactics that budget holders are finding the most difficult to achieve.

Exhibit 3.5 Abnormal seasonality and change between actual and budget.

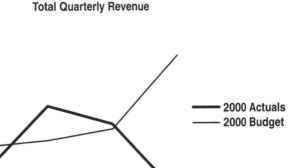

Total Quarterly Revenue

- What comments do budget holders have about the targets? List all comments entered by budget holders regarding what they feel can and cannot be achieved. These items may require further one-to-one collaboration if the plan is to be implemented.
- What metrics have changed the most since the last budget pass? Highlight those measures that have changed by a significant amount since the last pass. Where this occurs, the budget holder should have an explanation to support the change. If not, is the change realistic?
- Can this plan be funded? The summary financial statements will show projected cash flow and capital requirements. Are the projected returns worth the investment being considered?
- Could these results be improved? How do peer groups compare with each other? Who are the "good" and "poor" performers? Do any comments suggest improvements in performance could be obtained? Should any tactics be eliminated and their funding transferred to others?

The analysis for the last question may result in another budget pass. This would require communication of new pass objectives and any changes made to KPIs and top-down targets.

Threshold Planning. Although operational managers may work with only one tactical plan, the consolidated plan should store a range of threshold values for KPIs and other key metrics. These threshold values, whether good or bad, are used to trigger an alternative process if they are exceeded. For example, the cost of goods sold (COGS) may be budgeted at 15 percent. A lower threshold value of 13 percent and an upper value of 15.5 percent may be set. If these are exceeded, an alert is generated that causes the rebudgeting of those items affected by the measure. If a budget is not being achieved, there may be a case for reallocating resources from tactics that are not working to those that are. If a budget is being overachieved, the organization should question whether targets were too low (or market assumptions were incorrect) and should be set higher to maximize the plan's return.

Communicate

The purpose of this process is to transform strategy into reality. The communication process is unique in that it does not rely on systems, methodology, or metrics, although they can support the process. Putting strategy into action involves changing organizational behavior. Communication is the key.

Employees need to know what their role is in putting tactical plans into action and how they will be measured. Employees want to do a good job. When they have clearly defined goals and a clear line of sight to strategy, they will do a better job of setting priorities and making decisions in support of strategy.

Communication is made easier when employees have access to a company intranet on which plans and results can be published and updated. Some organizations arrange informative and motivational kickoff meetings at which plans are presented and employees are shown that CPM is a management system, not a stick with which to beat them. Whatever method is chosen, strategies and plans do not automatically become actions. To accomplish this transformation, managers must change and guide employee behavior.

Monitor

Typically, performance measurement and other types of control systems are used to determine whether resources are being properly allocated—

based on a comparison of actual to planned expenditures—and whether objectives and targets are being met—based on a comparison of actual results to planned results. However, organizations also should use these systems to determine the reasonableness of their resource allocations (the budget) and the ongoing validity of their strategic assumptions. Consider for a moment the two paths depicted in Exhibit 3.6. In this figure the dashed line from point A to point B represents planned results over a specified period of time. Recognizing that there will be minor deviations from plan, one might expect the actual results to deviate slightly from the targeted results. A deviation that is larger than expected typically is viewed as an operational error that needs to be corrected. However, what happens if the strategic assumptions are wrong, not the operations? What if the organization needs to change strategic direction toward point C, which could be a more effective alternative? The only way to make this sort of determination is to continually monitor the strategic assumptions on which the plan is based.

With CPM, monitoring consists of activities that review the financial plan, the tactical plan, and assumptions. Traditionally, the frequency of these reviews has depended on the industry and the organization's needs. For example, many companies adopt a monthly process for monitoring the financial plan, while those involved in high-volume manufacturing elect to monitor the tactical plan on a weekly or even daily basis.

Exhibit 3.6 Operational error, or bad assumption?

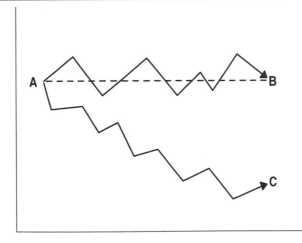

Corporate performance management systems support these regular reviews. However, they also support the automated monitoring of transactions and other business activities on an ongoing, real-time basis. When an exception occurs that threatens the implementation of strategy, the appropriate users are alerted. The system user can then conduct a full investigation.

As with any review, it is very easy for users to wander unguided through summary results, missing exceptions and opportunities hidden in the details. Efficient and effective monitoring requires focusing on the few significant variances rather than trailing through every exception for every customer, product, and market combination. A review methodology for monitoring actual variances, similar to the one set up for reviewing a budget pass, is important to the process. Analysis of variances, particularly those outside of the thresholds set during the budgeting process, may trigger other CPM processes.

Review Tactical Plan. This first activity reviews the success of the tactical plan and will help with the later review of the financial plan. The tactical plan should be reviewed in terms of actions taken by the budget holders and the analysis of exceptions. Actions taken should be supported by commentaries and associated KPIs detailed in the tactical plan—for example, the number of sales calls, the number of orders processed, the number of units made, and so on.

Where there is an exception (an unexpected KPI result), it is important to analyze the detail behind the measure. Not all measures will have supporting details, but where they exist, an investigation should take place at this lower level. If the KPI is related to customers, for example, then the analysis will rely on information supplied by the customer relationship management system. If the KPI is related to personnel, then the analysis will rely on information supplied by the sales order or human resources system.

Typically, the analysis should concentrate on trends over time and comparisons with peer groups. An example of a trend over time would be to review last year's performance versus this year's performance for specific products. Comparisons with peer groups might include displaying the performance of a salesperson with others or the performance of products in different geographic locations.

Review Financial Plan. Having looked at how well the tactical plan has been carried out, the next review should focus on the financial results ensuing from those actions. For most investors this is really what counts, so it is important to know where the plan has succeeded or failed. This review should focus on the cost of individual tactics and their impact on financial performance.

Review Assumptions.   In this final review step, the organization should appraise the basic assumptions made about the economic environment and how competitors are performing. Much of this external information can be obtained from corporate web sites and other public sources, government reports, and industry analysts. Without these sources, the data has to be either manually gathered or estimated based on experience.

Forecast

Accurate and objective business forecasts are critical to managing the implementation of strategy. Forecasting helps organizations, when necessary, make adjustments to tactical plans to achieve strategic goals. The process of forecasting involves predicting future results and evaluating either adjustments to existing plans or substituting alternative strategies. From this evaluation, informed decisions can be made and communicated about changes.

One of the biggest challenges to creating a forecast is removing bias and emotion that can affect accuracy. Because most products and services follow a typical adoption life cycle, statistical techniques can be used to minimize these challenges. By combining statistical trend analysis of measures supporting KPIs at a detailed level and operational knowledge of both the business and the marketplace, reliable predictions can be generated about the likely future outcome of current tactical and financial plans.

The two main types of forecasting are causal and time series. Causal forecasting assumes that, in addition to the data, other factors influence forecasts. For example, sales of a particular retail outlet will be affected by another store being opened in close proximity (store cannibalization). Time series forecasting relies solely on historical data and assumes that what has happened in the past will determine what happens in the future. Time series forecasting evaluates trends over time. It reveals the movement (trend), seasonality, and changes (variation) in the series being forecasted. Forecasting techniques evaluate each historical data series using a range of time-series models and select the best fit based on generated statistics for each series. From this information, forecast results are then generated.

When using statistical techniques, three points should be noted.

1. Aggregate forecasts are more accurate than individual forecasts. That is, looking at the total forecast for all products together will be more accurate than looking at any one particular product.
2. Long-range forecasts are less accurate than short-range forecasts. The next period is easier and more accurate to forecast than a period five years in the future.
3. Forecasts are never 100 percent accurate. Most forecasts are based on historical trends, and history never repeats itself exactly. Forecasts can be accurate but not precise or exact.

Despite these negatives, the value of statistical forecasts is that they cause users to think. If they know that their forecast will be assessed statistically, they are more likely to think carefully about the values and to be able, if necessary, to explain why their forecast is more accurate than the statistically generated one. Statistical forecasting also allows management to assess predictions without bias and emotion.

Once a forecast has been generated, it should be tested for statistical accuracy, such as detected seasonality and the goodness of fit. Forecasts outside a high level of confidence should be manually adjusted. Once complete, the resulting forecast should be compared with planned strategic goals, and any significant exceptions should be reported. These exceptions highlight areas that may affect future success of the strategic plan.

Based on the variances between the generated forecast and budget, changes to the tactical plan may be required. For example, it may be preferable to reduce the number of new product launches for the remainder of the year so that marketing resources can be allocated to those products having the most success. These decisions can be modeled in the scenario analysis process.

Report

The report process provides information to the various stakeholders who are not directly connected with implementing strategy. These groups include outside investors, government agencies, regulatory organizations, employees, and others. Those people involved with implementing strategy, such as operational managers, will have received the appropriate information from the monitor process to show their impact on strategy.

Reporting encompasses a number of activities, including adjusting, analyzing, and distributing. The "adjust" activity encompasses the preparation of the information gathered for reporting according to generally accepted accounting principles (GAAP). The "analysis" process includes producing key facts and figures on the nature of the business. Finally, results in the form of reports and analyses need to be distributed to those that need them.

In reporting to regulatory bodies or filing results on the stock exchange, it is essential to abide by the rules laid down by the various international accounting bodies. The adjust activity transforms results from internal accounting systems into those necessary for legal or statutory reporting. It provides the ability to change data and leave a record or audit of the change. This process supports the matching and elimination of intercompany trading, the elimination of minority interests, and other consolidation adjustments. Handling these requirements in a CPM solution allows management accounts to be tied to financial accounts and eliminates the need for additional systems.

The analysis activity takes information collected at each process and produces corporate performance reports for the various stakeholders. These reports consist of analyses by business activity over time and the outlook of performance in the future. Different users require different content and different levels of detail. Information from this process must be accessible to the other processes when required. For example, the latest actual and forecast will be required when replanning an activity.

Once produced, reports and analyses must be distributed to users of that information in the format most appropriate for them. For example, financial accounts will require annotations and commentaries for external publication, so the most appropriate format will be a text document. For a business analyst, a spreadsheet may be more appropriate because spreadsheets allow for the easy creation of additional analyses. A line manager may prefer a paper-based report or one that can be downloaded onto a personal digital assistant (PDA) for mobile access.

Feedback Loops

Corporate performance management processes are driven by feedback loops. These loops are triggered by an event, such as a forecast that indicates that the current tactical plan is unlikely to meet strategic goals. These events trigger the appropriate functions to replan or reassess tactics to achieve organizational objectives. Because every company is different, each organization should determine the feedback loops required by its own CPM processes. These feedback loops will help the organization become event driven instead of remaining calendar driven. The strategy formulation feedback loop and the plan and budget feedback loop are the most common.

Strategy Formulation Feedback Loop. The report process triggers the strategy formulation process when it shows that existing strategies are not working and indicates that another strategy needs to be deployed. The plan and budget process also may trigger the strategy formulation process when operational management is unable to develop tactical plans that meet strategic goals.

Plan and Budget Feedback Loop. After strategic goals are set or when the predicted performance from the forecast process is outside of the plan's threshold levels, the plan and budget feedback loop is triggered. The trigger may not necessarily be a numerical value. It may be an external catalyst, such as new government regulation, a new competitor appearing, or an event that causes organizations to focus on an environmental issue, such as the focus on security following the September 11 attacks. In these cases, management may induce the plan process to address these issues before they impact results.

Variances can indicate that the tactical plan has not been fully implemented or that some tactics either are not working or are costing more than planned. It also may be that the assumptions made during the plan and budget process are no longer true. Triggering the process for the affected areas may be able to correct this imbalance by reallocating resources.

SUMMARY

Chapter 1 illustrated how issues arising out of traditional processes contribute to the strategy gap. As shown in this chapter, CPM processes overcome these issues by:

- *Providing clear linkage to the strategic plan.* Each CPM process supports the implementation of strategy. These processes describe how strategy and associated tactics are to be put into action by operational managers. They also measure the success of those tactics in achieving strategic goals.

- *Introducing clarity and purpose.* Each process within CPM has a defined purpose. This purpose is clearly communicated to participants so that the right level of resources, time, and effort can be focused on achieving the desired results.
- *Using events to trigger change.* The implementation of strategy is a continuous activity. Exceptions encountered over time are used as the triggers for change to ensure tactical plans deliver the right strategic goals.
- *Presenting a market-based view.* The formation of strategy is greatly affected by external events. CPM processes capture external information and combine it with internal data to give an essential, holistic view of organizational performance in context of the market rather than just an internal perspective.
- *Focusing strategically instead of just tactically.* Financial measures based on the chart of accounts provide a focused view of performance that by themselves do not relate to activities required for strategy implementation. All CPM processes provide a broader view that looks at the performance of strategy and the resulting impact on financial results.
- *Providing early warnings.* Corporate performance management provides sophisticated forecasting capabilities that give an early warning of exceptions. This early warning allows users to evaluate possible corrective actions or to select alternative scenarios as required.

Endnotes

1. Nigel Rayner, Frank Buytendijk, and Lee Geishecker, *The Processes That Drive CPM*, Research Note COM-16-2849, Gartner, Inc., May 8, 2002, 1.
2. Ibid., 2.
3. Daniel H. Gray, "Uses and Misuses of Strategic Planning," *Harvard Business Review*, no. 86105 (January–February 1986): 89–97.
4. Gerry Johnson and Kevan Scholes, *Exploring Corporate Strategy*, 5th ed. (London: Prentice-Hall Europe, 1999), 104.
5. Ibid., 215.
6. Adrian J. Slywotzky, David Morrison, Ted Moser, Kevin Mundt, and James Quella, *Profit Patterns: 30 Ways to Anticipate and Profit from Strategic Forces Reshaping Your Business* (New York: Random House, 1999).

CHAPTER 4

Measurement and Methodologies

DOES MEASUREMENT MAKE A DIFFERENCE?

Cisco Systems is a worldwide leader in networking for the Internet. It provides networking solutions that connect the computing devices and computing networks making up the Internet and most of the corporate, education, and government networks around the globe. Cisco has been in business since 1984. In 1995 Larry Carter became Cisco's chief financial officer (CFO). At the time, Cisco took 14 days to close its books. By most measures this was considered better than average, but not to Carter. Cisco's revenue was growing at a compound annual rate of better than 60 percent. Worried that in 14 days a company with that rate of growth could "spin out of control," Carter set out to reengineer Cisco's financial processes.[1] By 1999 he had succeeded. The result was the "virtual close"—the ability to close the financial books within an hour's notice and to disseminate information instantly across their intranet. The system was highly touted not only by Cisco's senior management but also by the press and a variety of pundits, including the "big five" consulting firms. The system worked well until 2001. In the first few months of that year, Cisco failed to meet investor expectations. Its inventories doubled. In the third quarter of 2001, Cisco reported a loss of $2.69 billion. As their chief executive officer (CEO), John Chambers, noted, "This may be the fastest deceleration of any company of our size has ever experienced."[2]

What happened to the virtual close? It was supposed to give Cisco the ability to react instantly to changing market conditions. Chambers

Exhibit 4.1   Changes in financial performance before and after implementing a structured performance management system.

Financial Ratio	Average Before	Average After	Average Change
Total shareholder return	-5.1%	19.7%	24.8%
Stock return	-0.13%	0.18%	0.31%
Price/book value of total capital	0.03%	0.26%	0.23%
Real value/cost	-0.06	0.13	0.19
Sales per employee ($1,000)	98.8	193.0	94.2

provided one explanation when he said that, while the virtual close let Cisco look at the financial state of the company on a daily basis, it did not allow the company to predict the future, especially macroeconomic shifts.[3] Others attributed the failure to Cisco's culture (too growth oriented), its strategy (building inventory in anticipation of projected growth), its data (not all of the inventory data was automatically fed into its systems), and its partners (afraid to deliver news of the downturn in demand), to name just a few possibilities. Whatever the reasons, Cisco's experiences with its real-time financial system serve to underscore the complexities and potential problems associated with the successful design, creation, and deployment of any measurement system, even one as highly touted as Cisco's.

In spite of Cisco's downturn, some have suggested that the damage to the company would have been greater if it had not been using its measurement system. A variety of studies lend credence to this supposition. More specifically, studies indicate that organizational performance is enhanced by the implementation and deployment of a performance measurement system. For example, André de Waal reports that in 1998, researcher Edward L. Gubman did an analysis of 437 publicly traded firms, 205 of which had "structured" performance measurement systems. Based on his analysis, he found that over a three-year period, the financial performance of those firms with a performance measurement system was substantially improved by the deployment of those systems (see Exhibit 4.1) and the financial performance of those firms with a performance measurement system was substantially better than those firms without a system (see Exhibit 4.2).[4]

Exhibit 4.2 Financial performance of firms with
and without performance management systems.

Three-Year Growth Rates	Firms with Performance Management	Firms without Performance Management
Total shareholder return	7.9%	0.0%
Return on equity	10.2%	4.4%
Return on assets	8.0%	4.5%
Cash flow ROI	6.6%	4.7%
Real growth in sales	2.1%	1.1%
Real growth in employees	0.0%	1.1%
Sales per employee	$169,900	$126,100
Income per employee	$5,700	$1,900

These results are consistent with an earlier study by William Schiemann and John Lingle, based on an analysis of 58 companies that employed "measurement in a disciplined fashion" compared to 64 companies that did not.[5] The companies were asked to rate their performance on three criteria: whether their company was perceived as an industry leader, whether their company was financially in the top third of their industry group, and whether their most recent major change effort was successful. Their self-reported performance was later corroborated by data on their three-year return on investment (ROI). As the results in Exhibit 4.3 indicate, those companies with a managed measurement system substantially outperformed on all of the criteria those companies without a system.

Besides the financial payoffs, deployment of a performance management system also results in less tangible payoffs. Again, according to Schiemann and Lingle's study, measurement-managed companies have:

- Clear agreement on strategy among senior management (93 percent vs. 37 percent)
- Good cooperation among management (85 percent vs. 38 percent)

Exhibit 4.3 Relating measurement management to performance.

Measure of Success	Measurement-Managed Organizations	Non Measurement-Managed Organizations
Perceived as an industry leader over past 3 years	74%	44%
Reported to be financially ranked in the top third of their industry	83%	52%
Three-year return on investment (ROI)	80%	45%
Last major cultural or operational change judged to be very or moderately successful	97%	55%

Adapted with permission of The Free Press, an imprint of Simon & Schuster Adult Publishing Group, from *BULLSEYE! Hitting Your Strategic Targets Through High-Impact Measurement* by William A. Schiemann and John H. Lingle. Copyright © 1999 by The Metrus Group, Inc.

- Links between performance measures and company strategies (74 percent vs. 16 percent)
- Open sharing of information (71 percent vs. 30 percent)
- Employees willing to take a risk (52 percent vs. 22 percent)
- Links between individual performance and unit performance (52 percent vs. 11 percent)
- High levels of self monitoring by employees (42 percent vs. 16 percent)[6]

STATE OF THE MEASUREMENT ART

Underlying corporate performance management (CPM) is a performance measurement system. In Robert Simons's terms, a performance measurement system "assists managers in tracking the implementation of business strategy by comparing actual results against strategic goals and objectives. A performance measurement system typically comprises systematic methods of setting business goals together with periodic feedback reports that indicate progress against goals."[7]

All measurement is about comparisons. Raw numbers are rarely of much value. Knowing that a salesperson completed 50 percent of the deals he was working on within a month has little meaning. Now suppose

you know that the same salesperson had a monthly close rate of 30 percent last year. Obviously, the trend is good. Knowing that the average close rate for all salespeople at the same company was 80 percent indicates that this particular salesperson needs to pick up the pace. As Simons's definition suggests, the key comparisons in performance management revolve around strategies, goals, and objectives.

Goal-directed measurement systems have been around since the mid-1960s, with the publication of George Odiorne's *Management by Objectives: A System of Managerial Leadership.*[8] In management by objectives (MBOs), managers and their subordinates agree on a set of measurable objectives for their jobs as well as a timetable for their achievement. Managers and subordinates meet periodically to determine whether the subordinates are on target or not.

Today MBO is giving way to "management by fact," where the facts offer evidence of how well a company is doing with respect to corporate, business, and functional strategies, goals, and objectives. Unlike in Gubman's or Schiemann and Lingle's studies, researchers today would have a hard time finding a company that does not use a performance measurement system. The most popular system in use is some variant of Kaplan and Norton's Balanced Scorecard (BSC). Hackett Best Practices reports that 96 percent of companies have or plan to deploy scorecards over the next two years.[9] Among these companies, however, there seems to be some confusion about what constitutes "balanced."

The Balanced Scorecard Collaborative has established a set of criteria for certifying applications—software systems that provide Balanced Scorecard capabilities. In the words of the collaborative: "Central to the BSC methodology is [a] holistic vision of a measurement system tied to the strategic direction of the firm." It is based on four perspectives, with financial measures supported by customer, internal, and learning and growth metrics. "By measuring and managing the business using this holistic set of metrics, an organization can ensure rapid and effective implementation of strategy and facilitate organizational alignment and communication."[10]

Yet among the companies in the Hackett Best Practices study, the overwhelming majority of the measures are financial or operational in nature (better than 80 percent).[11] What the typical company really has is just a "scorecard"—a set of reports, charts, and specialized displays that enables it to compare actual results with planned results for a miscellaneous collection of measures.

In most companies, measurement practices are heavily "institutionalized," which means they are taken for granted and used in a mindless

Exhibit 4.4   How executives value and trust available information.

Measurement Area	% Who Value the Information	% Who Believe Measures Are Clearly Defined	% Who Say the Information Is Updated Regularly	%Who Are Willing to Bet Their Jobs on the Information Quality
Financial	82	92	88	61
Operational	79	68	69	41
Market/ Customer	85	48	48	29
People	67	17	27	16
Environment/ Community	53	25	23	25
Adaptability/ Innovation	52	13	23	16

Adapted with permission of The Free Press, an imprint of Simon & Schuster Adult Publishing Group, from *BULLSEYE! Hitting Your Strategic Targets Through High-Impact Measurement* by William A. Schiemann and John H. Lingle. Copyright © 1999 by The Metrus Group, Inc.

way. Calendar-driven financial reports are a major component of most performance measurement systems. This is no surprise for two reasons.

1. Most of these systems are under the purview of the finance department.
2. Most executives place little faith in anything but the financial or operational numbers.

This fact is amply demonstrated by results from the Schiemann and Lingle study cited earlier. According to their figures (see Exhibit 4.4), executives value a variety of different types of information, but they think that outside of the financial or operational arenas, most of the data are suspect, and 39 percent of executives are unwilling to bet their jobs on the quality of this information.[12]

The drawbacks of using financial data as the core of a performance measurement system are well known. Among the limitations most frequently cited are:

• Financial measures usually are reported by organizational structures (e.g., research and development expenses) and not by the processes that produced them.

- Financial measures are lagging indicators, telling us what has already happened—not why it happened or what is likely to happen in the future.
- Financial measures (e.g., administrative overhead) are often the product of allocations that are not related to the underlying processes that generated them.
- Financial measures are focused on the short term and provide little information about the longer term.

Financial myopia is not the only problem plaguing many of today's performance measurement systems in operation. Measurement overload and measurement obliquity are also major problems confronting the current crop of systems.

It is not uncommon to find companies proudly announcing that they are tracking 200 or more measures at the corporate level. It is hard to imagine trying to drive a car with 200 dials on the dashboard. Yet executives seem to have little trouble driving their organizations with 200 dials on the corporate dashboard, even though we know that humans have major difficulty keeping track of more than a handful of issues and that anything else is simply shoved to the side. A series of factors seem to be driving this corporate data overload:

- *Information fog.* Overall, the volume of unique information worldwide is doubling every year.[13] The digitization of information and nearly universal access to the Internet are the major forces behind this exponential growth. In 1999, approximately 1.5 exabytes (1 billion gigabytes) of unique information were produced. In 2001, the amount was 6 exabytes. The estimated cumulative total for all time is 21 exabytes. The trend shows no signs of diminishing. The bulk of this information is actually created and stored by individuals. We seem to have an insatiable need for information. Unfortunately, the tools for making sense out of these data have not kept pace.
- *Terabyte data warehouses.* A number of performance measurement systems are actually business intelligence systems built on top of data warehouses or data marts derived from these data warehouses. Over the years, these warehouses and data marts have become increasingly larger. Only a few years ago, terabyte (1,000 gigabytes) databases were a novelty. This is no longer the case. The largest decision-support data warehouse is now approximately 10 terabytes.[14] Armies of information technology staff are

devoted to feeding and nurturing these systems. The philosophy seems to be that since we have the capability to collect this information, we ought to be using it.

- *Data packrats.* Like boxes in an attic or shoes in a closet, organizations rarely retire the data they collect. If some new data or request for data comes along, it is simply added to the list. If the number of measures is 200 today, it will be 201 tomorrow. Even though plans change and opportunities and problems come and go with increasing frequency, little effort is made to determine whether the list of measures being tracked is still applicable to the current situation.

The second problem is something Michael Hammer has called the "principle of obliquity."[15] For many of the measures being tracked, management lacks direct control. On one hand, measures like earnings per share, return on equity, profitability, market share, and customer satisfaction need to be monitored. On the other hand, these measures can be pursued only obliquely. What can be controlled are the actions of individual workers or employees. Unfortunately, the impact of any individual action on a corporate strategy or business unit strategy is negligible. A strategic business model or methodology that starts at the top and links corporate goals and objectives all the way down to the bottom-level initiatives being carried out by individual performers is required to tie the "critical" with the "controllable."

EFFECTIVE PERFORMANCE MEASUREMENT

Any number of books provide a recipe for determining whether a collection of performance measures is good or bad. Among the basic ingredients of a good collection are:

- Measures should focus on key factors.
- Measures should be a mix of past, present, and future.
- Measures should balance the needs of shareholders, employees, partners, suppliers, and other stakeholders.
- Measures should start at the top and flow down to the bottom.
- Measures need to have targets that are based on research and reality rather than being arbitrary.

While these are all important characteristics, the real key to an effective performance measurement system is to have a good strategy.

71

Measures need to be derived from the corporate and business unit strategies and from an analysis of the key business processes required to achieve those strategies. Of course, this is easier said than done. If it were simple, most organizations would already have an effective performance measurement system in place, but they do not.

Andy Neely and others provide a good overview of the major processes involved in creating an effective performance measurement system.[16] Included among the processes are:

- *Design.* This involves the definition and selection of measures. The key is to measure what is right, not what is easy.
- *Plan and build.* This encompasses the planning of the support systems (including data collection and presentation) and the introduction of the measures and the system into the organization. This stage requires organizational change and overcoming organizational inertia.
- *Implementation and operation.* This involves the actual management by fact, using measures to monitor and analyze what is going on in the organization and its environment.
- *Refresh.* This involves the ongoing refinement of the measurement system to ensure that the measures remain relevant to the strategic direction of the organization.

While the first step is supposedly the easiest, it may be the most crucial. If the measures are poor, then the remaining steps will be ineffective. Toward this end, Neely and coauthors provide a template that can be used for defining the measures.[17] The template is reproduced in Exhibit 4.5.

Once a measure has been defined, it can be judged against a set of criteria to determine whether it is "good" or not. Several lists of criteria are available for this purpose. Jerry Harbour coined the acronym "SMART"—*s*pecific, *m*easurable, *a*ction-oriented, *r*elevant, and *t*imely— to represent his list of criteria.[18] Neely and others offer a 10-measures design test against which a measure could be compared. Included among the ten tests are: truth, focus, relevancy, consistency, access, clarity, so-what, timeliness, cost, and gaming.[19] The most comprehensive list is provided by Will Kaydos, who divided the criteria into two groups: efficiency and effectiveness. Kaydos's list, which is reproduced in Exhibit 4.6, can be used to judge new measures and existing measures as well as single measures and collections of measures.[20]

Exhibit 4.5 Measurement template.

Measurement Property	Explanation
Name:	What is it called and is it understandable?
Purpose:	Why is it being used and what action(s) is it encouraging?
Relates to:	What strategies does it support and what other measures is it linked to?
Metric/formula:	What is the actual measurement?
Target level(s):	What is the desirable level of performance?
Frequency:	How often is the measurement made and reported?
Source of data:	Where does the data come from?
Who measures:	What is the name and function of the person responsible for collecting, collating, and analyzing the data?
Who acts on the data (owner):	Who—name and function—is responsible for ensuring the performance levels?
What do they do:	How will the owner use the data and what actions can he or she take to improve performance?
Notes/comments:	

Source: *The Performance Prism: The Scorecard for Measuring and Managing Business Success* by Andy Neeley, Chris Adams, and Mike Kennerley. Copyright © Pearson Education Limited 2002. Reprinted with publisher's permission.

PERFORMANCE MEASUREMENT METHODOLOGIES

There is more to performance measurement than simply keeping score. An effective performance measurement system should help organizations:

- Align top-level strategic objectives and bottom-level initiatives.
- Identify opportunities and problems in a timely fashion.
- Determine priorities and allocate resources based on those priorities.
- Change measurements when the underlying processes and strategies change.
- Delineate responsibilities, understand actual performance relative to responsibilities, and reward and recognize accomplishments.

Exhibit 4.6   Key criteria for good measures.

Category	Criteria
Efficiency	Is all the data being collected actually being used?
	Are there easier ways to collect the data?
	Is there any duplication of collecting or processing data?
	Can the amount of data being collected be reduced by using sampling techniques?
	Can the frequency of collection or reporting be reduced?
	Can a measure be eliminated because it is no longer being used?
	Are there new tools that can be used to produce the information in another way?
Effectiveness	Are all key processes adequately measured?
	Are proper process measures in place to keep performance within acceptable limits?
	Is everyone getting the information they need?
	Does everyone understand the measures so they can interpret the results?
	Are users taking action as a result of the measures?
	Can the measures be easily used?
	Are the measures sufficiently timely and accurate?
	Does everyone have access to the information they need?
	Is the relative impact of different measures clear to users?
	Have the measures been changed to reflect change in processes?

Reprinted with permission from *Operational Performance Measurement* by Will Kaydos (Boca Raton: St. Lucie Press, 1999) 159–160. Copyright CRC Press, Boca Raton, Florida.

- Take action to improve processes and procedures when the data warrant it.
- Plan and forecast in a more reliable and timely fashion.

A holistic or systematic performance measurement methodology or framework is required to accomplish these and other aims. Over the past 40 or more years, various systems have been proposed. Some of these, such as activity-based costing, are more financially focused. Others, like total quality management, are more process oriented. In the discussion that follows, three approaches that support the basic processes underlying CPM are discussed.

Hoshin Planning

Hoshin is a strategic planning technique developed in the mid-1960s, around the same time as MBO. One translation for the term is "compass needle," reflecting its use in setting strategic directions. Hoshin grew out the total quality management (TQM) movement when Japanese managers realized that they needed a more comprehensive form of planning to manage major strategic changes. Hoshin enables management to create an annual (or semiannual) plan by helping them:

- Identify those areas where the organization can change or enhance its strategic vision.
- Determine the most effective ways in which to accomplish the change.
- Create a detailed implementation plan.
- Provide feedback mechanisms for monitoring and altering the plan.[21]

The stages of Hoshin planning are diagrammed in Exhibit 4.7. The stages follow the familiar TQM cycle of "plan, do, check or study, and act" and are very similar to more traditional forms of strategic planning. However, Hoshin planning is distinguished by its focus on a small set of vision "breakthroughs" (e.g., reduced cycle time) that can be accomplished in a reasonable period of time and that will enable the organization to move to the next level of success.

Several tools and techniques are available for executing the various stages of a Hoshin plan. One of these is Hoshin Kanri. The term "Kanri" means "management or control." This technique "provides a step-by-step planning, implementation, and review process for planning and managed change."[22] More specifically, it consists of "four coordinated matrices that document the organization's mission, strategies, objectives, goals, team activities, responsible parties, and associated measures." Each of the four matrices specifies and details the linkages between two of the major elements in a plan: mission to strategies, strategies to objectives,

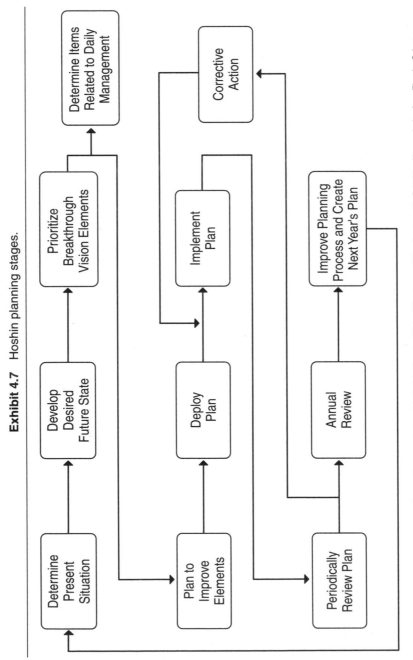

Exhibit 4.7 Hoshin planning stages.

Reprinted from *Beyond Strategic Vision: Effective Corporate Action with Hoshin Planning,* Michael Cowley and Ellen Domb, p. 21. © 1997, with permission from Elsevier Science.

objectives to goals, and goals to team activities. With Hoshin Kanri, the planning process proceeds in a stepwise fashion, specifying each of the four matrices in turn.

In the first step, the mission-strategies matrix is specified. Exhibit 4.8 displays a sample mission-strategies matrix.[23] Basically, this matrix indicates those strategies that are needed to accomplish particular elements of the mission. Here the rows of the matrix contain the elements of the mission (e.g., increase operational effectiveness), while the various strategies (e.g., manage material supplies effectively) are displayed as columns in the matrix. Each element of the mission has an owner, a weight indicating its relative importance among the other elements, a measure, a targeted value, and an actual value. Likewise, each strategy has an owner and a weight. At the intersection of each mission element and strategy is an icon specifying whether the relationship between the two is strong (triangle), moderate (square), or weak (circle).

Once the mission-strategy matrix is completed, attention is turned to strategies-objectives. This matrix delineates those objectives that are related to the various strategies in the plan. This matrix has the same structure as the mission-strategies matrix except that the strategies are now the rows and the objectives are the columns. The same is true for the objectives-goals matrix and the goals-actions matrix. The end result of the four steps is a cascade of linkages from the top-level breakthrough vision down to the bottom-level activities carried out by various organizational participants. The process ensures (at least on paper) that bottom-level activities are aligned with the strategic goals.

Balanced Scorecard

Probably the best-known and most widely used performance management system is the Balanced Scorecard. Kaplan and Norton first articulated this methodology in a 1992 *Harvard Business Review* article entitled "The Balanced Scorecard: Measures that Drive Performance." In 1996 they produced a groundbreaking book—*The Balanced Scorecard: Translating Strategy into Action*—that documented how companies were using the BSC not to only supplement their financial measures with nonfinancial measures but also to communicate and implement their strategies.[24] Over the last few years, BSC has become an almost generic term (much like Kleenex or Xerox) that is used to represent virtually every type of scorecarding application and implementation regardless of whether it is balanced or strategic. In response to this bastardization of

Exhibit 4.8   A sample mission-strategies matrix.

Mission vs. Strategies	Importance Rating (1-5 scale)	Manage Material Supplies Effectively	Manage Customer Expectations	Effectively Plan Manufacturing Resources	Develop and Improve Business Processes	Manage Finances	Create an Environment that Motivates	Improve Employee Morale	OBJECTIVE OWNER	MEASURE	ACTUAL	TARGET
Mission Increase Operational Effectiveness	4.0	△	△	○	△	□	△	△	Joe Scott	On-time Delivery	86%	78%
Create Stockholder Wealth	3.0	○	○	△	○	○	△	△	Sue Roberts	Return on Net Worth	13%	8%
Encourage Employee Development	5.0	△	△	○	○	□	△	△	Pete Smith	Emp. Opinion Survey	95%+	80%
Objective Owner		Fritz Meyers	Al Peters	Lilly Thomas	Earl Jones	Ken Tritz	Don Summer	Al Ogski				
Importance		90	90	54	60	18	108	108				

Strategies

Source: Becker Associates, Karen Becker.

the term, Kaplan and Norton released a new book in 2001—*The Strategy-Focused Organization*.[25] This book was designed to reemphasize the strategic nature of the BSC methodology.

From a high-level viewpoint, the BSC methodology is both a measurement system and a strategic management system. As a measurement system, BSC is designed to overcome the limitations of those systems that are financially focused. It does this by translating an organization's vision and strategy into a set of interrelated financial and nonfinancial objectives, measures, targets, and initiatives. The relationships among the financial and nonfinancial objectives are depicted in Exhibit 4.9.

The nonfinancial objectives fall into one of three perspectives:

1. *Customer.* These objectives define how the organization should appear to its customers if it is to accomplish its vision.
2. *Internal business processes.* These objectives specify the processes at which the organization must excel in order to satisfy its shareholders and customers.
3. *Learning and growth.* These objectives indicate how an organization can improve its ability to change and improve in order to achieve its vision.

The term "balanced" in a Balanced Scorecard arises because the combined set of measures is supposed to encompass indicators that are both:

- Financial and nonfinancial
- Leading and lagging
- Internal and external
- Quantitative and qualitative
- Short term and long term

As a strategic management system, BSC enables an organization to align its actions with its overall strategies. Like Hoshin planning, BSC accomplishes this task through a series of interrelated steps. The specific steps that are involved vary from one book to the next. Here the process is captured in five steps:

1. Identifying strategic objectives for each of the perspectives (about 15 to 25 in all)
2. Associating measures with each of the strategic objectives (a mix of quantitative and qualitative)
3. Assigning targets to the measures

79

Exhibit 4.9 Balanced Scorecard perspectives.

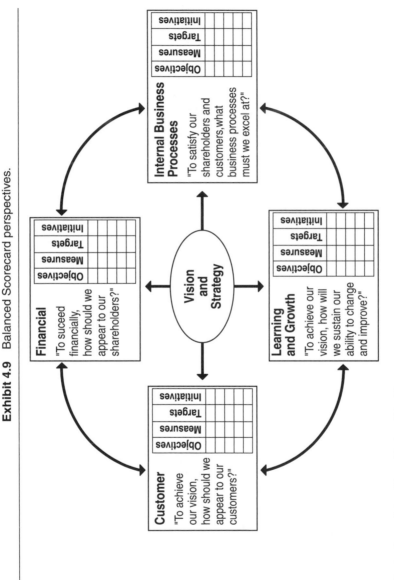

4. Listing strategic initiatives to accomplish each of the objectives (responsibilities)
5. Linking the various strategic objectives through a cause-and-effect diagram called a strategy map

As an example of the process, consider the strategy map shown in Exhibit 4.10. This map specifies the relationships among seven objectives

Exhibit 4.10   Sample Balanced Scorecard strategy map.

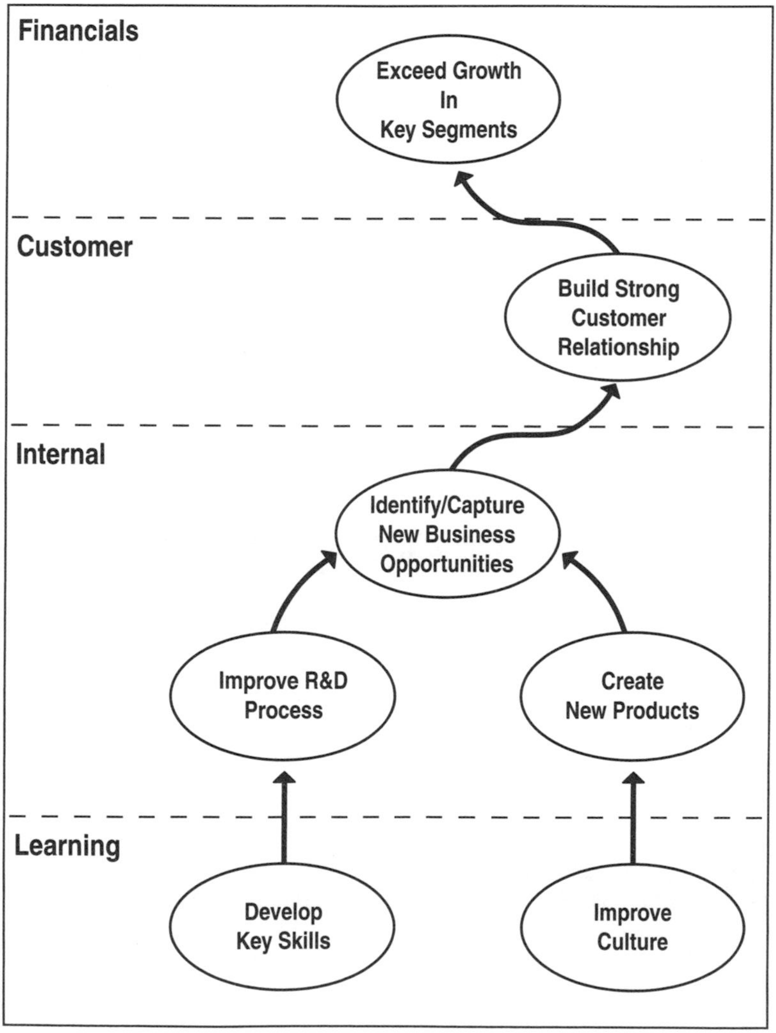

that cover four different perspectives. Like other strategy maps, this one begins at the top with a financial objective (e.g., exceed growth in key segments). This objective is driven by a customer objective (e.g., build strong customer relationships). In turn, the customer objective is the result of an internal (process) objective (e.g., identify/capture new business opportunities). The map continues down to the bottom of the hierarchy where the learning objectives are found (e.g., develop key skills).

Each objective that appears in a strategy map has an associated measure, target, and initiative. For example, the objective "build strong customer relationships" might be measured by "customer satisfaction." For this measure, an organization might target a 15 percent improvement over last year's figure in their customer service index. One of the ways of accomplishing this improvement is by "implementing the customer feedback database." The various components for this example are shown in Exhibit 4.11.

Overall, strategy maps represent a hypothetical model of a segment of the business. When specific names (a person's or team's) are assigned to the various initiatives, the model serves to align the bottom-level actions of the organization with the top-level strategic objectives. When actual results are compared with targeted results, a determination can be made about whether the strategy that the hypothesis represents should

Exhibit 4.11 Specifying objectives, measures, targets, and initiatives in a Balanced Scorecard.

Objective	Measure	Target	Initiative
What is the strategy trying to achieve?	How is success or failure against objectives monitored?	The level of performance or rate of improvement needed.	Key action programs required to achieve targets.

Objective	Measure	Target	Initiative
Build strong customer relationships	Customer satisfaction	Customer service index improves 15%	Implement customer feedback database

be called into question or whether the actions of those responsible for various parts of the hypothesis need to be adjusted.

Performance Prism

One of the major criticisms of the Balanced Scorecard is that it fails to take into account all of the major stakeholders that an organization faces in today's turbulent business environment. While the BSC framework incorporates shareholders (the financial perspective), customers (the customer perspective), and employees (the learning/growth perspective), it virtually ignores other stakeholders such as investors, intermediaries, alliance partners, suppliers, regulators, communities, pressure groups, labor unions, and the like.[26] Additionally, the BSC framework takes a one-sided view of the stakeholders it does consider. It only answers the question, What does the stakeholder need or want from the organization? and ignores asking, What does the organization need or want from the stakeholders? Consider objectives such as "customer loyalty" and "customer profitability." A little reflection suggests that these are things that organizations, not customers, want. Customers want fast, cheap, and easy-to-use products and services.[27] These two perspectives have substantial ramifications for the manner in which organizations formulate basic strategies and the measurements they use to monitor, analyze, and adjust these strategies.

The Performance Prism is a new framework designed to overcome the perceived limitations of the BSC. The framework is documented in a new book of the same name written by Neeley, Adams, and Kennerley. Instead of designing a performance measurement system around an organization's strategies, the Performance Prism focuses on the basic classes of stakeholders that an organization can encounter.[28] These include:

- Investors (shareholders and other capital providers)
- Customers and intermediaries
- Employees and labor unions
- Suppliers and alliance partners
- Regulators, pressure groups, and communities

The questions the framework attempts to answer encompass:

- *Stakeholder satisfaction.* Who are our stakeholders and what do they want or need?
- *Stakeholder contribution.* What do we want and need from our stakeholders?

83

- *Strategies.* What strategies do we need to put in place to satisfy these sets of wants and needs?
- *Processes.* What processes do we need to put in place to enable us to execute our strategies?
- *Capabilities.* What capabilities (people, practices, technology, and infrastructure) do we need to put in place to allow us to operate our processes more efficiently and effectively?[29]

The basic Performance Prism framework is shown in Exhibit 4.12.[30]

Another major difference between the Performance Prism framework and other performance measurement methodologies is its focus on processes. Among the key business processes to be considered are product and service development, demand generation, demand fulfillment, and enterprise planning and management.[31] Each process can be broken down into its subprocesses, which in turn can be broken down into their individual components (inputs, actions, outputs, and outcomes). For each of the processes, subprocesses, and individual parts, the potential questions to be considered by a performance measurement system are:

- *Quality.* How good?
- *Quantity.* How much?

Exhibit 4.12 Performance Prism framework.

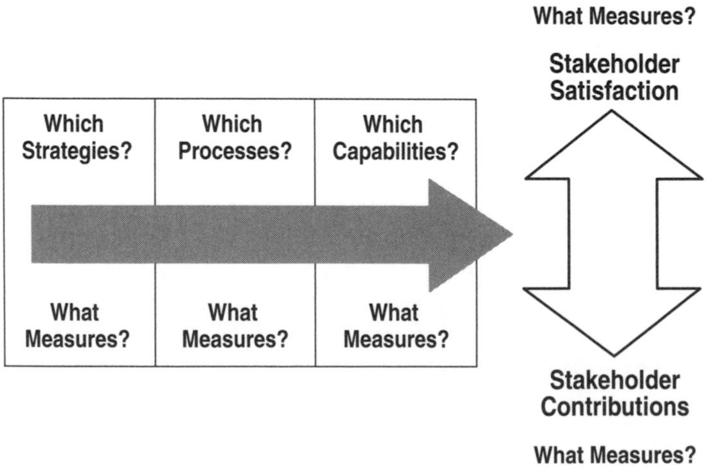

From *The Performance Prism*, by Andy Neely, Chris Adams, and Mike Kennerley.
© Pearson Education Limited 2002. Reprinted with publisher's permission.

- *Time.* How quickly?
- *Ease of use.* How simple?
- *Money.* How expensive?[32]

In a BSC, the linkages among the various objectives are displayed in a strategy map. In the Performance Prism framework, strategy maps are called "success maps." Success maps serve basically the same purpose, linking together the capabilities, processes, and strategies required to service or satisfy various stakeholder and organizational wants and needs. For any given want or need, the success map should cover all the facets starting at the bottom with capabilities, moving to processes, and then to strategies that are linked to the top-level wants or needs.

In addition to success maps, the Performance Prism promotes the use of "failure maps." A failure map is essentially a success map that asks, How can we reduce the risk of failure? For example, what sorts of strategies, processes, and capabilities would be needed to ensure that an organization's financial investors, customers, suppliers, or partners do not defect? Like a success map, a failure map starts at the bottom with capabilities that are linked to various processes and then links them to various strategies that can mitigate the risks and potential for failure.

SUMMARY

Reengineering a performance measurement system takes time and money. As with most reengineering projects, there is a tendency to put it off until tomorrow because the benefits are not readily apparent. While many of the benefits are longer term, data reported by Mark Graham Brown suggest that many benefits are more immediate and tangible.[33] Some of the benefits he has observed over the years include:

- As much as an 80 percent reduction in the volume of monthly reports generated by the finance function
- Over a 50 percent reduction in the amount of time senior managers spend in monthly meetings
- Up to a 60 percent reduction in the pounds of performance reports printed each day
- Elimination of up to an hour's worth of work spent each day by managers reviewing and interpreting performance reports
- Better balance between the focus on both short-term and long-term success of the organization

- Better balance in meeting the needs of all organizational stakeholders
- Better understanding among employees of the vision and values of the organization and better tracking of the achievement of the vision and values

Endnotes

1. Jim Harris, *Blindsided* (Oxford: Capstone Publishing Ltd., 2002), 140.
2. Ibid., 12.
3. James Cope, " 'Virtual Close' Fails to Work for Cisco," *Computerworld,* February 19, 2001.
4. André A. de Waal, *Quest for Balance* (New York: John Wiley & Sons, 2002), 24–25.
5. William A. Schiemann and John H. Lingle, *BULLSEYE! Hitting Your Strategic Targets Through High-Impact Measurement* (New York: The Free Press, 1999), 10.
6. Ibid., 12.
7. Robert Simons, *Performance Measurement & Control Systems for Implementing Strategy* (Upper Saddle River, NJ: Prentice-Hall, 2000), 7.
8. George Odiorne, *Management by Objectives: A System of Managerial Objectives* (New York: Pitman Publishers, 1965).
9. Hackett Best Practices, *2002 Book of Numbers: Strategic Decision-Making* (2002), 6.
10. Balanced Scorecard Collaborative, Inc., *Balanced Scorecard Functional Standards™ Release 1.0a,* May 5, 2000, 2.
11. Hackett Best Practices, *2002 Book of Numbers: Strategic Decision-Making* (2002), 11.
12. Schiemann and Lingle, *BULLSEYE!,* 40, 47.
13. Harris, *Blindsided,* 78–79.
14. Richard Winters, VLDB Survey, 2001, www.wintercorp.com/VLDB/2001_VLDB_Survey/winners/table1.html.
15. Michael Hammer, *The Agenda* (New York: Crown Business, 2001), 106.
16. Andy Neely, Chris Adams, and Mike Kennerley, *The Performance Prism* (London: Pearson Education Limited, 2002), 32–33.
17. Ibid., 35.
18. Jerry L. Harbour, *The Basics of Performance Measurement* (Portland, OR: Productivity Press, 1997), 39.
19. Neely, Adams, and Kennerley, *The Performance Prism,* 45.
20. Will Kaydos, *Operational Performance Measurement* (Boca Raton, FL: CRC Press, 1999), 159–160.

21. Michael Cowley and Ellen Domb, *Beyond Strategic Vision* (Newton, MA: Butterworth-Heinemann, 1997), 17.
22. Becker Associates, *Strategic Planning Using Hoshin Kanri,* 2001, www. becker-associates.com, 2001.
23. Becker Associates, www.becker-associates.com, 2001.
24. Balanced Scorecard Collaborative, *Balanced Scorecard Functional Standards™ Release 1.0a,* 5.
25. Robert S. Kaplan and David P. Norton, *The Strategy-Focused Organization: How Balanced Scorecard Companies Thrive in the New Business Environment* (Boston: Harvard Business School Press, 2001).
26. Neely, Adams, and Kennerley, *The Performance Prism,* 159.
27. Ibid., 167.
28. Ibid., 166.
29. Ibid., 160.
30. Ibid., 161.
31. Ibid., 171.
32. Ibid., 173.
33. Mark Graham Brown, *Keeping Score* (Portland, OR: Productivity Press, 1996), 13.

CHAPTER 5

Corporate
Performance
Management Systems

IMPACT OF TECHNOLOGY
ON THE FINANCE FUNCTION

So far this book has explored key corporate performance management (CPM) methodologies, metrics, and processes. This chapter reviews the final CPM component: technology systems.

Technology systems—and their impact on the finance function and performance management—have changed dramatically over the last half century. Extensively developed for military use during World War II, computers only really became available for commercial applications in the 1950s. IBM, probably the most influential manufacturer in those early years, developed machines specifically to support business applications such as billing, payroll, and inventory control, which at that time were manually intensive processes that restricted organizational growth.

By the 1960s most major organizations were using computers for many of their accounting functions, primarily the recording of financial transactions and the monitoring of stock. But these machines were expensive and had limited functionality. For example, computers could perform only one task (payroll) for one user at a time. Systems could not support multiple users or multiple applications simultaneously. As a result, computer power was inaccessible for finance staff involved in planning and budgeting, and these processes remained manual tasks. But things were about to change.

Time-Sharing

The development of new operating systems and improved hardware led to the creation of time-sharing, eliminating the problem of one task for one user. With time-sharing, a computer could perform multiple tasks for multiple users at the same time. However, these specialized computers were expensive, and the cost was difficult to justify within a single organization. Commercial time-sharing companies emerged to solve this problem by developing computer networks that, for a connection fee, allowed organizations to share a computer with other companies.

Time-sharing companies targeted departments within organizations that were not supported by their own internal information technology (IT) departments but had a need for computing power. To make their offerings more attractive, these companies developed operating systems and applications designed specifically for nontechnical end users. Finance departments became an early target with applications designed to support planning and reporting processes.

Departmental Solutions

As the use of computer technology soared, so did the cost. Operating systems for in-house systems could only be rented. The alternative, time-sharing with a specialist company, was addictive, and usage often went unchecked. A solution to these spiraling costs was the development of the departmental computer. Here, a small computer was purchased complete with an operating system and associated software, and was dedicated to a department. Digital Equipment Corporation (DEC), which was subsequently taken over by Compaq Computer Corporation and then by Hewlett-Packard, was very successful in targeting finance departments. DEC provided a way of both controlling computing costs and giving finance staff the power they needed to operate more efficiently.

Personal Computers and Spreadsheets

The next major breakthrough for finance was in the early 1980s with the combination of two technologies: the spreadsheet and the personal computer (PC). Although PCs had been around for a few years, they had made little impact on finance departments. Similarly, spreadsheet-type applications had been around on mainframe computers for some time, but they were expensive to buy and few users had access to them.

In 1979, a "killer application" for finance was born: a spreadsheet program called VisiCalc. VisiCalc was initially available on Apple Computer machines and then, in 1981, on IBM PCs. For a relatively low cost compared with mainframe computer hardware and software, finance departments could now develop their own planning, budgeting, reporting, and analysis applications without having to wait or disturb a busy, stressed-out IT department.

The impact on finance of this application's introduction was enormous, and sales of PCs for corporate use rose sharply. VisiCalc was followed by Lotus 1-2-3, which became the spreadsheet of choice in the early 1990s. It was replaced by Microsoft Excel when Microsoft Windows became the standard operating system for corporate PC systems. Today spreadsheets are probably the most popular productivity tool available to accountants because of the freedom they provide in planning and analyzing results.

Online Analytical Processing Technology

Online analytical processing (OLAP) also had a major impact on finance. The term "OLAP" describes a set of analytical capabilities and, quite often, the technology that supports those capabilities. Although the term only came to prominence in the mid-1990s, the technology has been around for over 25 years and is well known in IT circles.

Online analytical processing generally provides the system user with the capability to change the view of a report. While the content of rows and columns are fixed in a standard spreadsheet, users can swap rows and columns around at will in an OLAP system. Unlike a report that provides only a single view of the business, hence the need for hundreds of reports, OLAP is flexible enough to provide a user with as many different views as are required in a simple, intuitive way. Users have a quick and unrestricted way of navigating through a lot of information, while at the same time eliminating the need for IT departments to write, maintain, and run hundreds of reports that probably will go unread.

The term "dimension" is used by OLAP systems to describe a particular point of view. For example, the "organization" dimension would contain information about different departments and the way in which they are related in a hierarchical structure. Another dimension would be the accounts to be planned and reported. Time, such as months and years, would represent a third dimension. In an OLAP system, these different dimensions can be swapped quickly and easily by dragging the appropriate dimension either across or down the screen. Pivot tables in Microsoft Excel provide similar capabilities.

What has made OLAP so successful with finance departments in recent years has been the availability of systems designed to be set up and maintained by nontechnical people. In a matter of hours, finance staff can set up sophisticated business models that can support planning, budgeting, and general-purpose analysis applications.

Enterprise Resource Planning

Perhaps the most recent major impact of IT on finance occurred during the late 1990s with the introduction of enterprise resource planning (ERP) systems. ERP improved the efficiency of organizations by linking multiple processes to a common database (see Exhibit 5.1). This linkage also improved the integrity of results because there was now only one version of a particular piece of information. A data change in one process automatically affected information in a related process. While it was not easy to implement these complex systems, the design of these integrated solutions has greatly impacted organizations and software vendors alike. No one today looking for a back office system would

Exhibit 5.1   ERP systems link multiple processes to a central database.

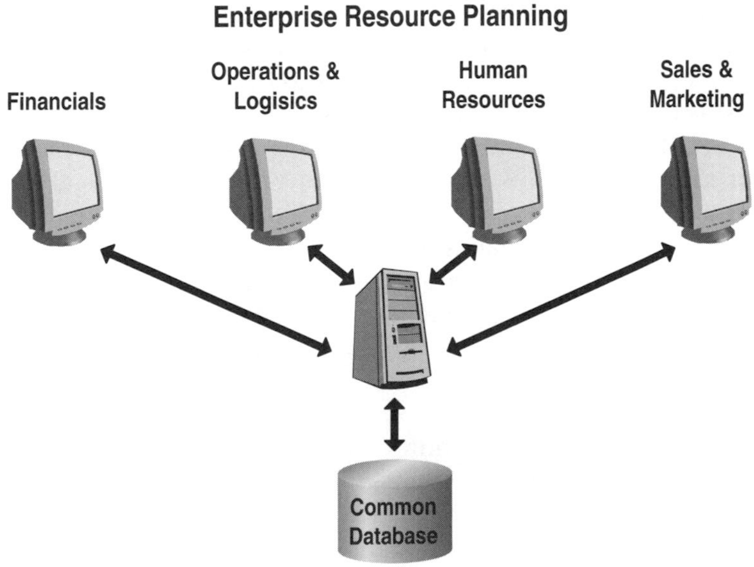

Enterprise Resource Planning

| Financials | Operations & Logisics | Human Resources | Sales & Marketing |

Common Database

implement discrete, separate solutions for accounts payable, accounts receivable, and stock. It does not make sense because these activities are closely related, and a change in one impacts the others. Organizations implement these functions as a single transaction-based system. Similarly, software vendors of these solutions no longer offer separate applications; they only offer integrated solutions, although they can be purchased as modules.

Efficiency and Effectiveness

Technology developments have transformed the way in which finance is seen and the way in which the finance department carries out its role in today's organizations. Over the last 50 years, many of the developments have improved the efficiency of how organizations record and report their transactions. But, while efficiency is always important, a more pressing need today is for finance organizations to be more effective. After all, what is the point of having systems that enable the planning, budgeting, and reporting processes to happen more quickly, when the result is still a process that does not help the company more effectively implement strategy?

With the systems knowledge and experience gathered over the past five decades, one might logically expect finance departments to be the models of efficiency when it comes to automating processes using information technology. Unfortunately, this does not seem to be the case. Hackett found in its benchmark study of strategic decision-making that, on average, only 25 percent of organizations fully use technology to perform consolidations and online analyses, and only 20 percent fully use technology for performance management.[1] The reason given for this lack of usage despite the high visibility of ERP and analytical applications is the fragmented approach that organizations take, which results in multiple systems and data stores that are not integrated. As a result, getting access to consistent information in a way that supports the different CPM processes is difficult, time consuming, and beyond the limited resource capabilities of many organizations. If so few organizations actually can access and analyze information properly, on what are the rest basing their decisions? For most, it seems to be gut instinct when too little—or too much—information is available.[2] When it comes to effectiveness, much room for improvement remains.

Faced with this lack of efficiency and effectiveness, many organizations today are looking for ways to improve their planning and reporting capabilities. Industry analyst group IDC has measured the market size for business performance management applications, which encompass CPM, and estimates that the demand for cross-functional applications that evaluate and measure the success of business strategy will grow at an annual compound growth rate of 10.8 percent from 2001 to 2006.[3]

In a recent survey conducted by Comshare, organizations reported that the major reason for considering new planning and reporting systems was to improve their analysis capabilities. But analysis by itself does not lead to the implementation of strategy. Unless it is combined with the planning, budgeting, and forecasting of strategic initiatives, analyses provide little assistance in overcoming the strategy gap.

CHARACTERISTICS OF CPM SYSTEMS

The role of a CPM system is to facilitate the implementation of strategy. To do this, CPM systems take advantage of the technology developments of the past 50 years to overcome the issues discussed in Chapter 1 that contribute to the strategy gap. Whereas traditional solutions treat each part of the CPM process in isolation, CPM systems provide support as a single closed-loop system. Users can move from planning and budgeting to forecasting to reporting at any time, in the same system, and using the same interface. As with ERP, administrators have a single system to maintain, a single set of business rules to apply, and a single repository of information from which to draw, no matter where users are located or where they are in the CPM process.

Traditional systems also cause the strategy gap in that they are focused on past performance based on the chart-of-accounts view of the organization. Corporate performance management is about managing performance to produce future results. To that end, CPM systems focus on the future with their strong capabilities in forecasting and evaluating alternative courses of action. In performing these functions, CPM systems handle all types of information, not just financial. They cope with statistics, user comments, and documents from a variety of sources, both internal and external to the organization.

Capabilities

All CPM systems do far more than simply collect and report numbers. The systems exist to support users through the various processes in implementing and monitoring strategy and to provide a single window through which all users of an organization view business performance on all aspects of the company.

Like the car in the road analogy from Chapter 1, a CPM system is a tool for traveling down the business path. The design and capability of the system will determine how effectively an organization travels.

When driving down a road, particularly one that constantly changes direction and produces surprises in the form of unforeseen objects in the path, drivers cannot spend time monitoring the status of the car itself. Instead they must concentrate on the road, relying on warning systems to tell them when the vehicle needs attention, such as when it needs more fuel or is overheating.

In the same way, CPM systems have automated processes that allow those managing the company to focus on the direction and to implement change quickly. In addition to providing basic capabilities that can help the organization adjust its direction, CPM systems are designed to highlight the unexpected by providing warnings when actual or predicted direction deviates from plan. To achieve this level of performance, CPM systems have nine characteristics:

1. *Offer complete integration.* CPM systems encompass planning, budgeting, forecasting, financial consolidation, reporting, and analysis, and treat them as a single, continuous process. They support senior management in the evaluation, selection, and communication of strategic initiatives. They support operational management in the development of tactical plans and assist budget holders in assigning money, people, and assets to chosen initiatives to achieve corporate strategic goals. CPM systems highlight tactics that are working and those that need attention. They allow end users to create their own reports, investigate the causes of exceptions, and assess the impact of proposed changes.

2. *Are enterprise wide.* CPM systems are extensible across the enterprise and provide a collaborative infrastructure for the different CPM processes to take place around the globe. CPM systems are web based, making it possible for users to work from anywhere at any time. Users are no longer tied to a specific machine or location.

3. *Focus on exceptions.* CPM systems accommodate the reporting and analysis of both financial and nonfinancial data because the success of strategy is not measured in monetary units alone. They focus users' attention on the unanticipated by highlighting and

proactively alerting them to exceptions, eliminating the need for users to search through stacks of reports. And once an exception is found, CPM systems allow users to drill down into the detail so they can see what is really happening.

4. *Automate the processing of data.* CPM systems automate the processing of ratios, currency conversions, allocations, elimination of minority interests, the consolidation of results, and more.

5. *Filter and format data.* The human ability to take in information only through eyes and ears greatly limits the amount of data that can be absorbed. CPM systems summarize large volumes of data and present it in a form that is easily understood. Examples include creating financial documents such as the income statement, the balance sheet, and the cash flow statement from the detailed chart of accounts, and providing supporting analyses.

6. *Provide end users with access to information.* The web has transformed the way in which we obtain information. It allows us to access information in disparate systems, at different locations, and in different formats anytime, anywhere. All CPM systems exploit the web and provide secure user access to any relevant information, such as timetables, assumptions, comments, reports, analyses, actuals, and forecast results. Information is easy to access and navigate online.

7. *Support collaboration.* All CPM systems are designed with collaboration in mind. They support existing collaboration facilities such as e-mail, instant messaging, and bulletin boards, meaning that, for the first time, users can collaborate with colleagues no matter where they are or what time it is.

8. *Provide insight.* One of the main purposes of a report is to reveal something that was previously unknown or unexpected. However, if information is presented purely as a page of numbers, spotting trends and exceptions within the sea of data can be difficult. Corporate performance management systems overcome this by providing strong analytical capabilities such as trend analysis, sorting, charting, and exception reporting, transforming data into insight.

9. *Provide automated monitoring of vital signs.* Reports have a number of limitations. For example, they are static, accurate only at the exact time they are produced, and tend to consist of summarizations that mask problems lurking in the detail. All CPM systems, in contrast, are "live," searching the underlying details on a continuous basis. They proactively warn users when exceptions

occur and highlight issues that would otherwise be hidden in summarized reports.

By combining these characteristics, CPM applications become a powerful management system. They allow executives to assess and communicate strategy; provide operational management with tools for developing effective plans; and give end users instructions and knowledge on how to perform their roles in implementing strategy. Be warned, however: Although CPM systems may improve efficiency, they cannot ensure effectiveness by themselves. They are only as good as the methodology, metrics, and processes that they support. Often organizations believe that by implementing a new system they will solve their planning, budgeting, reporting, or analysis problems. If the planning or other processes are broken, a new system will not fix them. The result will still be a broken process.

ARCHITECTURE OF A CPM SYSTEM

Components

The term "application architecture" refers to both the logical and the physical design of an application. The logical design details an application's functional elements and their interactions. The physical design specifies how the logical design is actually implemented and deployed across a specific set of technologies, such as desktops, servers, databases, communication protocols, and the like. This chapter is concerned with the logical design.

As mentioned earlier, CPM systems can be thought of as the vehicle that takes an organization from where it is to a destination farther down the road. This vehicle is an integration of individual components, each of which is vital but relatively useless if not integrated as a complete package (see Exhibit 5.2). Provided that the driver knows how to operate the vehicle and where to go, three major components in the vehicle contribute to the success of the journey: the chassis onto which everything is bolted, the engine which drives the vehicle forward, and the controls used to steer and regulate the vehicle. The design and integration of these components as a whole is critical to the drivability of the vehicle and will determine how effectively the occupants reach their objective. In addition, for the vehicle to move, it requires a constant supply of good-quality fuel.

Exhibit 5.2   Like a car, a CPM system relies on
integrated components to perform its function.

	Car	CPM Systems
Client Tier (User Interface)		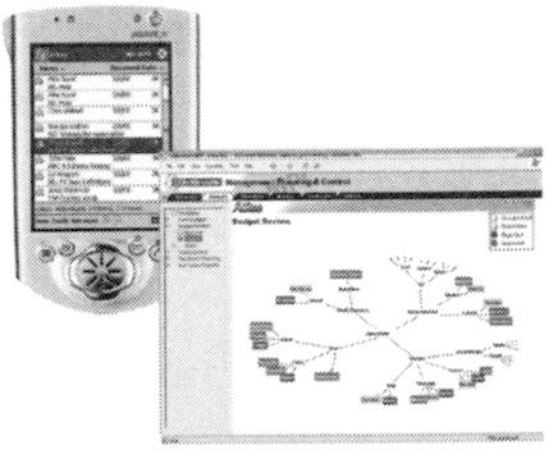
Application Tier (Process Functionality)		 Budget, Report, Forecast...
Data Tier (Data Model)	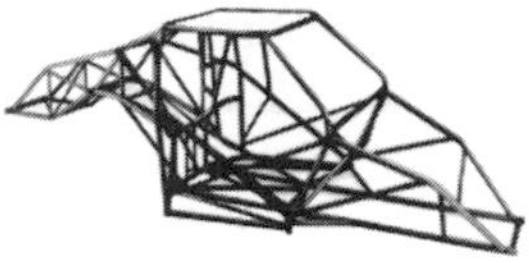	
Data Source		 ERP General Ledger

Similarly, a CPM system is an integration of individual components, each of which is vital but relatively useless if not integrated with the others. To contribute to the successful implementation of strategy, a CPM system consists of three layers or tiers: a data tier, an application tier, and a client tier.

The data tier is the chassis of a CPM system. It contains a definition of the organization covering the past, present, and future and is expressed in terms of structures and business rules. It also contains information, or links to information, in the form of plans and results. It is on this data model that the other components of a CPM system operate.

The application tier is analogous to a car's engine. This tier powers the CPM processes by transforming user interaction and source data into plans, reports, and analyses according to preset rules and operator selections.

The client tier is used to steer and regulate the implementation of strategy through communication, collaboration, and guidance of user interaction. It also monitors the success, direction, and progress of strategic initiatives and provides warning of real and potential problems as well as opportunities.

For the CPM system to operate, it requires a constant supply of good-quality data. That data will be supplied from a variety of internal sources, such as the enterprise resource systems (ERP), human resources (HR), and customer relationship management (CRM) databases as well as from external sources such as news agencies, market research, and public listings.

The design and integration of these components in technology terms is known as the application architecture. The way in which these work together is critical to the effectiveness of a CPM system in helping employees, managers, and senior executives implement strategy.

Application Architecture

The architecture of a CPM system affects what that system can do, how well it will scale as more users come online, and the amount of effort that will be required to maintain it. The technology features and functions used in the solution can be the best in the world, but unless they actually fit and complement each other well, the resulting system is substantially less than the sum of its parts.

Consider spreadsheets. On the surface, they seem ideal for planning, budgeting, and reporting. Setting up models is fairly straightforward and something that most nontechnical people can do. Spreadsheets offer many functions and provide a user-friendly interface for formatting, sorting, and charting results. However, the architecture—the way in which these capabilities have been put together—makes it practically impossible to implement an enterprise-wide budgeting and reporting system.

One limitation is that only one person at a time can use a spreadsheet. To accommodate many users, multiple spreadsheets need to be developed for each person, which then must be linked back into a central spreadsheet. This duplication leads to integrity problems. The person responsible for collecting results can never be sure that everyone is using the latest version and that the results they see on their consolidated sheet are the same as those held by individual users.

A second limitation is that spreadsheets support only one view of the business unless pivot tables are used. If pivot tables are used, setting up rules and templates for controlling the data-gathering process becomes very difficult. A typical spreadsheet model has accounts listed down the sheet as rows and time periods listed across the sheet as columns. Because of this fixed view, it is cumbersome to customize data entry and reports so that they reflect only those measures that the user is responsible for. It is also extremely difficult to produce a report that shows any other layout, such as revenues by product, region, and strategic initiative.

Another issue is that actual data is held in a variety of other systems, such as the general ledger. Getting data into the spreadsheets and then distributing them to users can be difficult and time consuming. Data must be mapped into the appropriate cells and spreadsheets, which again must be customized for each user to prevent them from seeing data belonging to other users. Once updated, the spreadsheets must be distributed, which for a multiple-user system can be an enormous task.

Because spreadsheets are designed for general-purpose analysis, cell rules do not automatically recognize the difference between a debit and credit value or the different account types, such as profit and loss, balance sheet, or statistical ratio. Knowing the difference is essential when it comes to consolidating data and creating variances. For example, creating a better/worse variance requires the system to understand the account type because simply subtracting one number from another will not necessarily give the right result. Similarly, when aggregating data over time, as is done when creating an annual total, balance sheet and ratio accounts cannot be summed, and ratio accounts will need to be recalculated. Because of this lack of understanding of account types, setting up business rules in spreadsheets is complex, as the rule for each cell needs to be carefully considered, which then makes subsequent maintenance difficult.

Spreadsheets also are limited in the amount of data they can hold and, therefore, require multiple files to hold just one set of data. When organizations multiply this by the number of files required to support each user, they quickly understand why creating an efficient, effective, enterprise-wide system is all but impossible.

The problems caused by spreadsheets are well documented. Studies by KPMG and Coopers and Lybrand revealed that over 91 percent of the spreadsheet-based systems they investigated contained errors.[4]

Why is it that one of the world's leading productivity tools is so inept at supporting CPM? The answer is simple: The architecture was never designed to support enterprise-wide CPM. When choosing a system to support CPM, it is important to specify one with the right architecture. The remainder of this chapter focuses on the key technology requirements of a CPM system.

CPM DATA TIER

Data Model Design Options

The CPM data tier houses a model or models that hold information about the way in which the organization operates. In IT terms, this is known as metadata. This information includes measurement definitions, account attributes, organization units, hierarchy structures, and currency conversion methods. This model also will hold or reference data from all parts of the CPM process, such as strategic and tactical plans, assumptions, competitor and market share information, comments, top-down targets, budgets, forecasts, and actual results.

This data tier can be designed in a number of ways. Industry analyst Gartner identifies four of them:

1. *Direct connections to the underlying operational data stores.* In this instance, the model does not hold data but rather directly accesses the data source, such as the general ledger. Although this design provides up-to-the-minute information, the disadvantage is likely to be poor performance because the CPM system needs to access the various data sources continually. These data sources will be optimized for transaction processing, not the query processing required by the CPM system. The queries also could impair the performance of the underlying operational system. Another problem with this design is that it lacks any historical context because data always are reflected as current values.

2. *Use of an operational data store.* With this design, the CPM system itself is implemented directly on top of an operational data store, such as the general-ledger database. While it would help with performance, this design could be costly to develop because the operational data store database would need to be extended to accommodate information not held naturally. Examples of this type of information include tactical plans, competitor information, assumptions, and key performance indicators (KPIs). This additional development would complicate the maintenance of the operational data store. Like the direct connection option, this approach provides only limited historical context because structures and definitions would be those that are current.

3. *Use of a dedicated data mart and data model.* This design involves the setting up of a dedicated data model that has a dedicated data mart attached to it. This data mart is fed with source data from the underlying operational systems. This design is relatively quick to implement and typically performs well. This is the approach adopted by many of the specialist and business intelligence (BI) vendors that currently provide CPM solutions. One disadvantage of this design is that it may not support real-time updates and monitoring. In addition, the technology may not be capable of being leveraged across other BI applications.

4. *Use of an enterprise data warehouse and data model.* This fourth design, favored by many ERP vendors, consists of a data model that accesses a general-purpose data warehouse. The benefit is that this design would serve as the platform for other BI applications and would provide consistent, high-quality data. The downside to this approach is that it can be an expensive option if the data warehouse does not yet exist, and it can require significant time to implement.[5]

Successful Designs

The preferred design choice is the one that best aligns the data infrastructure and investment decision with the top-down strategic objectives and return on investment requirements of the enterprise. Many successful early adopter implementations use the third design option, which involves a dedicated CPM data mart and data model. In this design, both data and metadata are held in a central database to which everyone attaches. This is very similar to the design used in today's ERP systems. Unlike file-based and traditional discrete systems, data and metadata is held only once and can be shared across all processes. This greatly simplifies maintenance and eliminates integrity issues caused by duplication of systems and data.

The CPM data models have sophisticated security systems that restrict access to functionality and information that can be viewed. Users interact with their data only, while managers see all the data for their area of responsibility.

Typically, a CPM data model consists of a number of separate data stores for specific types of financial and nonfinancial information (see Exhibit 5.3). A summary financial data store houses the data and results used to generate management and financial reports. One or more supporting stores that focus on a specific activity—for example, customer and sales activity—will be linked to this summary data store. To preserve integrity, this data is dynamic. As the supporting store is updated, the summary results automatically populate the summary store. Holding different data stores within the same database is sometimes referred to as a multicube design.

Exhibit 5.3   A CPM database encompasses a number of data sources (multicube design).

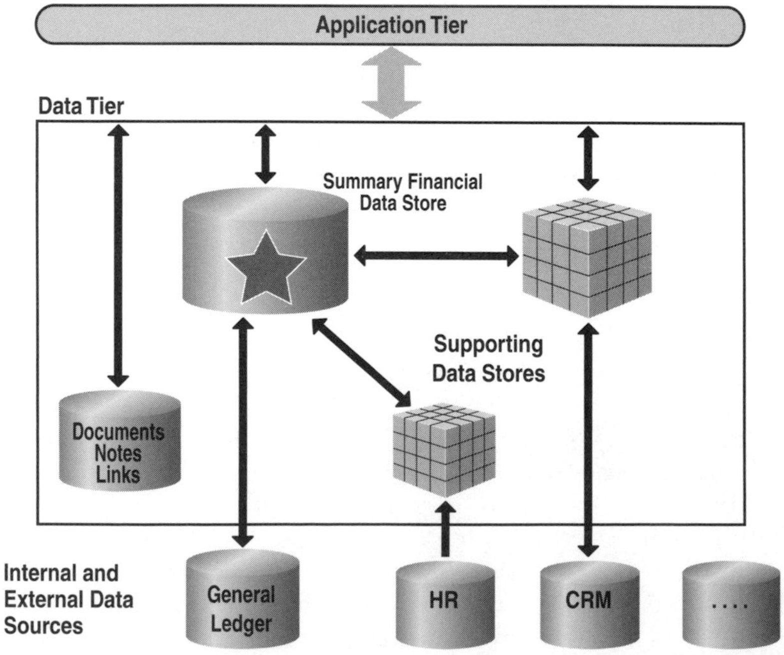

Data stores are fed from underlying transactional systems, but the links to the underlying data stores are retained. Therefore, when querying a value in the CPM system, users can access the transaction that generated the result. In this way, CPM systems become the main interface to any information on performance.

Separating these data stores provides a number of benefits. It simplifies the setup and maintenance of the data model. When dealing with financial results, for example, the data store will require a business dimension for the legal entities and their structure over time. When looking at sales information, the data store needs to hold information by product, customer, and perhaps location. Human resources information may need to be held by operational unit. Not all dimensions (e.g., year, region, and product) apply to all data items, and not all members (e.g., 2002, West, and widgets) will apply to all data stores. Keeping the data stores separated makes maintaining the model easier for the administrator but does not detract from the "single-view" operation of the system.

Separating the data stores also allows the CPM system to be optimized for performance. Each data store of a CPM model will have specific characteristics that can be tuned. For example, the financial data store will need to recognize the financial attributes of an account, while a customer-focused data store may contain only sales information. Knowing that only certain types of accounts exist in certain data stores, plus knowing which dimensions apply to which data stores, enables users to choose the appropriate technology for each data store and to finely tune the performance of the overall application.

In addition, the separation of data stores allows for easy growth of the application. Continuous development is characteristic of CPM models; they never start out with all the pieces in place. Having separate data stores allows for an initial CPM application to be focused on a particular requirement, such as budgeting by department, while allowing it to be easily expanded later, such as adding customer reporting with a data store sourced by the CRM system.

Attributes of CPM Models

All CPM systems are fundamentally different from traditional systems used for planning and reporting. These CPM systems have a number of attributes that enable the creation of a realistic model that can be used throughout the CPM process. When combined, the following attributes describe the physical capabilities of a CPM system. These attributes, which are essential to strategy implementation, include multidimensional focus, common business rules and common data, built-in financial intelligence, unrestricted rule access, and time intelligence.

Multidimensional Focus. "Multidimensional" describes the way in which numerical information can be categorized and viewed. For example, consider the number 57. The number must be defined to have meaning. In this case it is revenue. It could be further described as having occurred in the West region in the month of June for the year 2002. To define it further, 57 could be described as an actual result for product X. This example describes six aspects of the number 57. These are known as "dimensions" (see Exhibit 5.4). The values of each aspect are known as "members" of the relevant dimension. Dimensions often have multiple members.

All CPM systems are multidimensional; that is, they fully support OLAP (see Exhibit 5.5). Each piece of information held by the model is qualified in terms of a dimension and the appropriate member of that dimension.

But what makes a CPM system special is its flexibility. When viewing information, for example, the user can determine at will which dimensions are shown across and down the screen. The user can also "nest" dimensions. In Exhibit 5.6, each version dimension (2003, 2007) includes multiple nested members (actual, budget, and forecast). Similarly, the account dimension has been nested within the product dimension.

Exhibit 5.4 Information in a CPM system is qualified
in terms of dimensions and members.

Dimension	Member
Account	Revenue
Region	West
Month	June
Year	2002
Version	Actual
Product	X

Exhibit 5.5   CPM systems are multidimensional,
fully supporting online analytical processing.

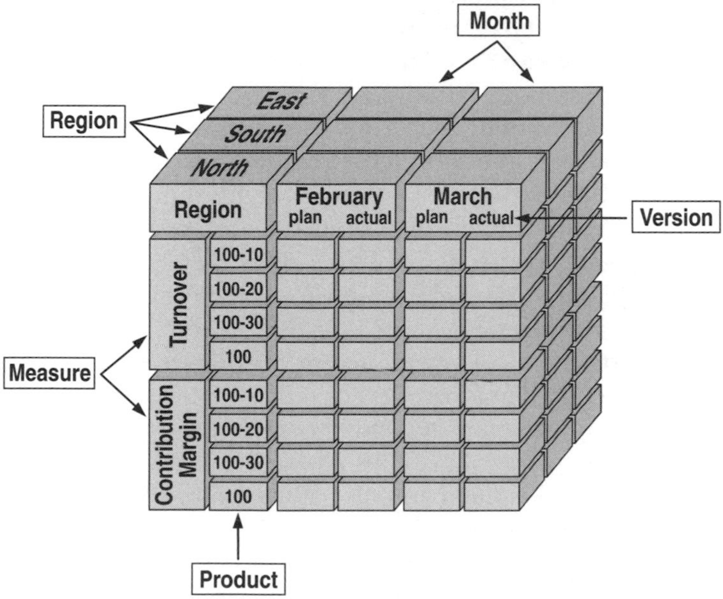

Exhibit 5.6   Multiple dimensions and members.

	2003			2007		
	Actual	Budget	Forecast	Actual	Budget	Forecast
Product 1						
Income	25,000	20,000	25,000	20,000	25,000	20,000
Cost of Goods Sold	21,500	18,000	21,500	18,000	21,500	18,000
Other Costs	700	700	700	700	700	700
Contribution	2,800	1,300	2,800	1,300	2,800	1,300
Product 2						
Income	18,750	11,250	18,750	11,250	18,750	11,250
Cost of Goods Sold	16,125	10,875	16,125	10,875	16,125	10,875
Other Costs	525	525	525	525	525	525
Contribution	2,100	-150	2,100	-150	2,100	-150
Product 3						
Income	5,750	5,750	5,750	5,750	5,750	5,750
Cost of Goods Sold	4,945	4,945	4,945	4,945	4,945	4,945
Other Costs	161	161	161	161	161	161
Contribution	644	644	644	644	644	644

Users can swap these dimensions around at will without help or support from an administrator. This allows data to be viewed in the most suitable context for the job, such as the comparison of results over time, with peer groups, and by version.

CPM data stores are defined by dimension. For example, the members of the organization unit dimension are defined independently of the account, time, version, and product dimensions. Members also can have relationships assigned to them. For example, the Total Company member would be defined as the total of the other divisions, which themselves are totals of individual units. In this way, the data store can hold product and organizational hierarchies that also can be consolidated. These hierarchical dimensions support alternative hierarchies to cope with the different structures that may prevail, such as legal and management structures. They also cope with different versions of the same structure to accommodate reorganizations. For example, this year, last year, and proposed management structures can be held and used on the single version of raw data. This allows historical results to be preserved in a historical context and also allows comparisons between the current and proposed structures.

The accounts dimension contains formulae that describe how to calculate measures such as contributions, totals, and ratios. These formulae may differ between versions so that, for example, revenue can be calculated from units and price for budget purposes, while price is calculated from revenue and units when reporting actual.

This separation of dimensions and members greatly simplifies application setup and maintenance. All CPM models allow huge numbers of dimensions and an almost limitless number of members in each dimension, allowing them to cope with the most complex of organizations.

Common Business Rules and Common Data.   All CPM models have a common set of dimensions, dimension members, and business rules, although, as mentioned above, those rules may be specifically restricted to specific versions and processes. As a result, one change in a structure or member automatically updates all associated reports and analyses.

Similarly, only one set of base data is held even though there may be multiple structures and versions of structures in operation. This means that a specific number is held only once, whether it appears in the strategic plan, the budget, or actual results. This attribute eliminates the time and effort in moving data or updating rules in multiple systems. It also greatly improves integrity because only one version of the truth is ever held.

Built-in Financial Intelligence. All CPM models have built-in financial intelligence that automatically understands the different types of measures when processing data. Accounts can be defined as both financial and nonfinancial. Measures such as ratios will not be consolidated. Nonfinancial measures such as headcount and volume will not be converted to a base currency.

The CPM model distinguishes between profit and loss (P&L) and balance sheet accounts. The model then uses this information to correctly calculate year-to-date totals in both reports and ad hoc analyses.

The understanding of debit and credit assignments is essential for any financial account. This information is used in reports and ad hoc analyses to produce correct better/worse variance reporting.

Some measures may be defined as "opening balances." Built-in financial intelligence enables CPM models to automatically populate these from the appropriate closing balances. This is an essential requirement when forecasting or planning into the future.

Often there is a need to support multiple currency perspectives for global planning and reporting. CPM models are able to translate accounts at different rates, detect and calculate exchange gains/losses, and then consolidate results into a base or multiple base currencies. The more sophisticated CPM models are also able to convert measures at multiple sets of rates, such as budget and actual rate, enabling the comparison of results to assess the impact of exchange fluctuations.

Different CPM processes require different levels of detail. For example, strategic plans may occur at a divisional level, budgets at a departmental level, and actuals at a level wherein results are collected by product or customer. Where the level of detail coincides, CPM systems allow the direct comparison of data.

The embedded financial intelligence of a CPM model saves time and effort in the setting up and subsequent maintenance of a system. It ensures that end users have the right answers when they prepare their own ad hoc reports and analyses.

Unrestricted Rule Access. Business rules can be assigned to measures that are able to access values in any other measure and in any other dimension and dimension member combination. This capability allows the setting up of allocation rules that, for example, spread the total cost of the marketing department across all sales cost centers, based on the volume of product that was budgeted by each. Another use of this capability allows the setting up of central drivers that can be used by budget holders—for example, the calculation of revenue by taking the volume sold by each sales department and multiplying it by the price entered by the marketing department.

To evaluate these kinds of rules correctly, the CPM model must be able to perform multiple passes of the model. In the previous allocation example, the model first must calculate the total cost of the marketing department before it can allocate the cost, which then will require a second consolidation. These rules can be recursive: that is, the result of a rule may be used by itself in a second pass of the same rule. Without this capability, the CPM model would not be able to cope with allocations, the calculation of minority interests, and the generation of cash flow statements.

Time Intelligence. Another attribute of a CPM model is that it understands the concept of time. It supports financial accounting cycles of any length. For example, budgets may be entered monthly, cash flows generated quarterly, and actual results reported weekly. Where time matches between versions of data, the model will allow direct comparisons.

A CPM model also can hold data for any length of time both in the past and in future years, to enable historical comparisons and trend analysis. In addition, it can accommodate the relative referencing of time. For example, when reporting the last six months, the CPM model will know how to roll over to last year when reporting data in the first quarter of a new year.

All CPM models can generate year-to-date figures without having to write rules. These summations automatically handle the correct treatments of P&L and balance sheet accounts.

To reduce maintenance time, CPM models also have an indicator of the current period. This indicator is used to determine the focus of any report. For example, if a report shows the current month and last month, setting the indicator to "May" will tell the model to automatically show results for May and April. Built-in time intelligence makes CPM models much easier to set up and helps organizations cope with the move toward continuous planning.

Data Model Technologies

The database technology used to implement a CPM data model can be multidimensional, relational, or a hybrid of both. Each has unique characteristics and needs to be chosen carefully to match the organization's requirements. However, regardless of the technology selected, users should be allowed to choose, where appropriate, the way in which information is displayed down and across the screen or page.

Multidimensional Databases.   Multidimensional databases were developed to overcome the limitations of relational databases. Relational technology initially was developed for IT departments to support transaction processing and record keeping. Due to the lack of calculation capabilities, there was little or no support for viewing data in a multidimensional way or for creating organizational models that reflected the different business dimensions. In contrast, multidimensional databases were designed specifically to ease the setting up of business models and to enable interactive multidimensional analysis.

In a multidimensional database, data is stored in "cubes" that combine the various business dimensions of an organization. Leading vendors in this space include Applix, with its TM1 database, and Hyperion, with Essbase. Interestingly, Oracle used to be the market leader with its product, Express, but Oracle recently dropped this product in favor of a relational approach.

The advantages of multidimensional databases are that they perform extremely well in complex data analysis and are relatively easy to set up and maintain. The disadvantages are that they are number based and need additional technologies to handle information in text and date form, which is essential for CPM solutions. They also lack standards, meaning that many applications featuring multidimensional databases are proprietary. At best, the organization has to learn a new technology to maintain or extend the application. At worst, it means the organization is forever at the mercy of the database vendor in providing updates and new functionality to allow the organization to retain a competitive advantage with its IT infrastructure.

Relational Databases.   Relational databases have been around for over 30 years and are common in every organization. They underpin the general ledger, ERP, CRM, and HR systems and are used by IT departments to create customized systems. Vendors such as Microsoft with SQL Server, Oracle, and IBM with DB2 dominate the industry. Their products can be found in most organizations. Because of the prevalence of relational databases, standards have emerged that all vendors comply with in terms of updating records and providing access.

In a relational database, information is stored in relational tables rather than in cubes. Tables are two-dimensional in that they consist of records, and each record consists of fields or columns (see Exhibit 5.7).

Exhibit 5.7 Relational database star schema.

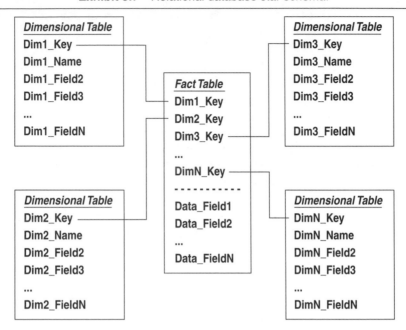

The number of fields is fixed for each table. A relational database can consist of many tables that can have different numbers of fields. Multidimensional analysis is achieved by creating a number of tables containing specific fields that are related. This type of design is known as a star schema or snowflake schema.

A star schema consists of a central fact table with a multipart key that holds data and results and a set of smaller tables called dimensional tables. Each dimensional table contains a key and dimensional members along with their attributes. For example, a location dimension table would contain a set of records defining specific locations. An individual dimension table is joined to the fact table through its key, which is also part of the multipart key in the fact table.

In the past, the disadvantage of the relational approach was poor performance due to the complex queries required to mimic the functionality of multidimensional cubes. However, use of star schemas combined with the dramatic performance improvements in relational technology has transformed the way these applications perform. For many organizations, the performance is comparable to multidimensional technology. The strength of relational databases lies in their openness, that is, their ability to integrate with other systems, such as the general ledger and ERP systems. Another strength is their scalability, that is, the ability to support hundreds of users with large volumes of information. Openness and scalability are two key requirements in the deployment of CPM solutions.

Hybrid Solutions. In recent years, relational vendors, particularly Microsoft, Oracle, and IBM, have developed multidimensional capabilities within their relational products. Microsoft, for example, offers Analysis Services with SQL Server 2000. This product is multidimensional in appearance and maintenance but uses relational technology to store data and metadata. Oracle 11i and IBM DB2 OLAP Services provide similar capabilities.

These technology leaders have recognized that organizations need both relational and multidimensional capabilities but prefer them to be combined in a single technology. This combination frees organizations from potential integration and maintenance issues. By using a hybrid approach from a single vendor, users benefit from the performance and reduced setup time of multidimensional technology and from the openness and scalability of relational technology. Given this move toward hybrid solutions by the major database vendors, it seems that pure multidimensional technology products will be confined to niche markets in the very near future and may even die out altogether.

CPM APPLICATION TIER

Integrated Processes

The application tier of a CPM system consists of functionality that turns data stored in the CPM model into plans and results. As discussed in Chapter 3, a CPM system must manage and support the core CPM processes of strategy formulation, scenario analysis, tactical planning, budgeting, communication, monitoring, forecasting, and reporting. The CPM application tier must fully integrate these processes, allowing organizations to focus on implementing strategy and avoid the strategy gap. All CPM systems also help organizations to become event or trigger based rather than calendar based. The checklists shown in Exhibits 5.8 through 5.14 outline the base CPM system functionality required to support each core process.

Exhibit 5.8   Situation analysis and strategy checklist.

Situation Analysis and Strategy Formulation Functionality Checklist

Strategy Formulation

❑ Create financial model based on centrally defined business dimensions.

❑ Integrate actual, forecast, and historic data from a central database for modeling purposes.

❑ Model information based on strategic initiatives.

❑ Driver-based modeling—for example, the ability to enter a driver such as an inflation rate that uplifts all relevant data.

❑ Link strategy text with resulting goals to allow publication of the strategic plan.

Scenario Analysis

❑ Top-down goal setting that allows a total to be entered that then adjusts the underlying data.

❑ View, side by side, various scenarios in order to evaluate and choose the right combination of strategies.

CPM CLIENT TIER

The client tier consists of the user interface through which users gain instruction and interact with CPM processes. It must be designed carefully to meet a range of different user needs. For example, management needs to be able to communicate objectives, goals, and timetables, and review results. Users need guidance through the various CPM processes. Additionally, users must be able to communicate with management on

Exhibit 5.9   Planning checklist.

Planning Functionality Checklist

❑ Development of tactical plans linked to strategic goals.

Exhibit 5.10 Budgeting checklist.

Budgeting Functionality Checklist

Revenue, Expenses, and Capital Planning

❏ View strategic plan text and goals, budget timetable, and budget-pass objectives.

❏ View actual, forecast, and top-down goals by strategic initiative.

❏ Generate a seeded budget based on historical extrapolation.

❏ Enter data against targets by strategic initiative and other relevant business dimensions.

❏ Spread annual amounts based on seasonality and other relevant profiles.

❏ Plan salaries by employee, groups of employees, title, and grade. Includes entering percentage amounts, bonuses, and more by date to generate periodic amounts without user involvement.

❏ Plan assets by asset type, group, and more. Should include the automatic calculation of depreciation and book value based on asset criteria.

❏ Calculate and post allocations.

❏ Attach text and notes to entered numbers.

❏ Support user-defined planning that can take place at a lower level than defined by the CPM model, such as budgeting advertising by publication when only a total advertising account has been specified in the CPM model.

Plan and Budget Review

❏ Support an approval process where users enter plans and submit them to managers who can reject or approve. Standard facilities include the reporting of approval status and the integration of email capabilities to warn users when submissions have been submitted, approved, or rejected.

❏ Lock plans once approved to prevent unauthorized changes.

❏ Automatic alerting of plans or budgets that exceed set targets.

❏ Reporting and charting capabilities that highlight inconsistencies in submitted plans. Inconsistencies could include, for example, phasing that is different from previous years, an abnormal jump between the end of the last actual period and the start of the new budget period, and a budget that is substantially different from a statistically generated budget.

❏ Review of budget and management comments during the process.

❏ Generate comparative information including income, balance sheet, and cash flow statements.

Exhibit 5.11 Communication checklist.

Communication Functionality Checklist

❑   Deliver online access to detailed tactical plans incorporating budget goals and supporting text.

Exhibit 5.12 Monitor checklist.

Monitor Functionality Checklist

❑ Load data from transaction and other systems, both internal and external, which feed the CPM system.

❑ Employ email to automatically alert managers to actual results that differ from budget thresholds.

❑ Allow drill back to the detailed transactions from a summary report item.

❑ End-user analysis on any exception including the ability to show that exception in the context of last year, last month, as a trend, and with peer groups.

Exhibit 5.13 Forecast checklist.

Forecast Functionality Checklist

❑ Time series analysis of key accounts, using the resulting formulae to predict future performance. Typical capabilities include ignoring exceptional one-off results in the data to be trended, and some form of control over any significant growth or decline. The analysis should show the goodness of fit and, if required, allow the rejection of forecasts where there is a low statistical probability of achieving the forecast.

❑ Automatic alerting where predicted results differ from the budget thresholds set in future periods.

❑ Modeling and evaluation of changes to individual tactics that may result in a revised budget being set for certain tactics or budget centers.

Exhibit 5.14   Report checklist.

Report Functionality Checklist

❑ Match, eliminate, and audit inter-company accounts.

❑ Adjust results with audit trails for the financial accounting treatment of minority and other related adjustments.

❑ Audit interrogation of results in sufficient detail to pass external audit scrutiny.

❑ Automatic generation and distribution of results to individual users via printer, website, and e-mail.

the ability to meet or exceed targets and must be able to comment on results and issues that affect them. Because enterprise-wide systems contain so much information, the CPM user interface needs to focus users' attention on what is important so they can take action early.

User Access Methods

The way in which users access the CPM solution will vary depending on their location, their degree of expertise, and what they want to do once they have access. For many users, the web is ideal for delivering a CPM solution. This medium has done a great deal to help standardize access to information by providing a common, simple, and intuitive method that eliminates the need to know about the technicalities and location of the underlying system. However, the web by itself is not the complete answer for all users. For instance, a CPM system that requires users to be online to access information may not be that useful when the user is traveling. Also, for users creating reports, the web offers relatively few formatting capabilities. These users also may need to add information to provide the right context for their communication. Here, the spreadsheet and word processor are the best tools for adding context. For these reasons, CPM systems need to provide a wide variety of access options for both online and off-line users.

Web Browser.   The web browser is the primary tool for accessing information in a CPM system. Web-based systems are extremely efficient when it comes to broad deployment across the enterprise. Adding more users is a simple matter of sending the user the appropriate URL address. There is no need to load or maintain software on a user's machine. The web allows continuous changes to be made to the CPM system without having to go through any arduous rollout process.

When using a web browser to access information, users are freed from a machine or location, meaning they can access a CPM system anywhere, anytime. Web browsers can deliver text and formatted numbers, handle the interaction with functions, and contain links to other related documents. All users access the same version of the data, which eliminates version control issues and data controversies. Changes to a web-based system are communicated instantly to all users without the need to send files, templates, or anything else.

Spreadsheets.   Spreadsheets are probably the most popular accounting tool due to their formatting and analytical capabilities. Today's spreadsheet programs, such as Excel, are very sophisticated in that they also can act as a window on top of a database, provided that capability has been enabled. For an example, see Exhibit 5.15. This means that data can surface—or appear—directly in the cells of a spreadsheet and then can be

Exhibit 5.15   Today's spreadsheets can act as windows to databases.

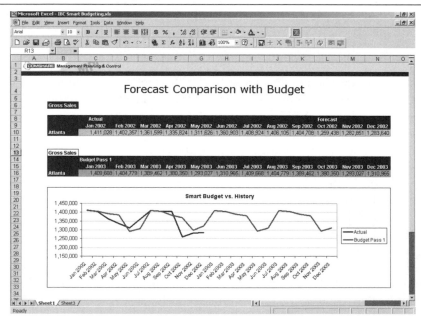

Exhibit 5.16   PDAs are being used for the
delivery and updating of CPM information.

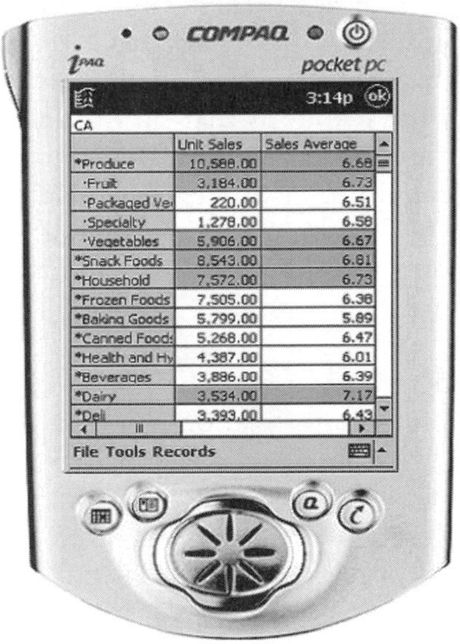

used in other calculations and reports. In this way, users can exploit their spreadsheet skills to produce highly formatted reports and analyses, but the underlying data still are coming directly from the CPM database.

Using a spreadsheet in this way also allows mobile users to disconnect from the main CPM system and take relevant information with them on the road. Many systems allow users to update these spreadsheets off-line and then submit changes to the CPM database when they next go online.

Portable Devices.   In recent years, the usage of personal digital assistants (PDAs) has grown dramatically. Initially, PDAs were used to provide contact and calendar information. But with the increasing sophistication of devices coupled with wireless communications and automatic synchronization capabilities, PDAs are replacing PCs for some users. Some CPM systems now support these devices for the delivery and updating of corporate performance management information because of the benefits they offer (see Exhibit 5.16). They can be carried anywhere easily. Information is available immediately without a lengthy boot-up process. They provide both online and off-line access to data, allowing synchronization with a central corporate system through existing phone connections.

Role of Analytics

The way in which the interface presents information is critical because more information is available today for decision making than at any other time in history. Left unassisted in this environment, users can waste time looking for exceptions that do not exist or that cannot be found because they are buried within a sea of data. All CPM systems overcome this by highlighting critical exceptions through a range of analytical and visualization techniques that include color-coding, sorted lists, hierarchical exceptions, detailed exceptions at a summary level, and the use of software agents.

Color-Coding. Color-coding is used to help draw users' attention to performance areas that need investigation. A column or row of numbers can be color-coded according to some simple rule, such as "show all numbers less than minus 5 in red, between minus 5 and positive 10 in yellow, and above 10 in green." This color-coding can be taken a step further in that the value can be portrayed pictorially. For example, values may be represented as sections of a map, with various portions of the map being color-coded.

Sorted Lists. Even with color-coding, the user still has to look through the list to find exceptions. By producing a sorted list, such as "show the top 10," the user now only has to look at the top of the report to find the exceptions.

A sorted list offers three benefits.

1. It makes it almost impossible for the user to miss the exception because the most important information is presented first.
2. A sorted list reduces the volume of data the user has to view, saving time and effort.
3. Because of this reduced volume, the amount of "bandwidth" (a term denoting the speed of access) required to support users is also reduced. This is an important point when connecting across countries where Internet access is slow.

Hierarchical Exceptions. Hierarchical exceptions reveal exceptions in the context of their position within a structure. For example, Exhibit 5.17 illustrates actual budget margin variance by product. The "All products" dimension, seen in the center, includes "stereos," "speakers," " tele-

Exhibit 5.17 Hierarchical exceptions capture exceptions in the context of their positions within structures.

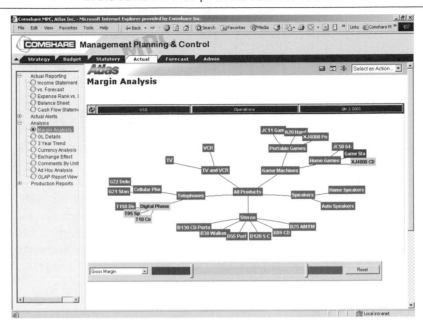

phones," and more. The products are divided up further within each of these members.

The coding of each variance is shown in relation to where it fits within the product hierarchy. This type of display helps users to evaluate whether the exception involves the entire entity (telephones), or a portion of it (Digital Phone T95 SP). In the example shown, the user can click on a member and drag it to rotate the hierarchy, revealing all parts of the structure. Those members that are not in focus can still be seen as color-coded dots. In this way, it is possible to view and understand thousands of exceptions quickly.

Detailed Exceptions at a Summary Level. Often summary reports can mask detailed exceptions. For example, if one budget center misses its goal by 5,000 but centers within the same division exceed their goals to the same extent, the entire division will appear to be within budget. In a CPM system, the color-coding for the division would show the division being within budget overall but would place a symbol alongside the division to show that a detailed unit was outside of the acceptable limit, prompting further investigation. When a user clicks on the symbol, the detailed variance is presented. By employing detailed exception reporting, hidden exceptions do not go undetected, and time is not wasted searching each hierarchy for exceptions that may not exist.

Software Agents. Because business is changing so rapidly, organizations rely on CPM systems to provide proactive alerts to bring exceptions to their notice without having to search and analyze reports. Software agent technologies do this searching automatically without the user even needing to be present.

When an exception is found, the software generates an alert, often in the form of an e-mail that is then sent to the appropriate user. Upon opening the e-mail, the user can select the alert and view the place in the database that generated the alert. Exception rules can be quite sophisticated, such as "generate an alert when sales for three consecutive months have decreased, while at the same time advertising expenditures have increased." Like warning systems in a car, this means users will be alerted only when there is an issue that needs immediate attention, instead of having to spend time monitoring results.

Once an exception has been highlighted, CPM system users can—security permitting—access data online in any time period or version without advance notice. Reports do not need to be preconfigured. Users are able to view and analyze data across any appropriate dimensions, without limitations, such as by initiative, product, line of business, and so on. They are able to rotate and nest dimensions as well as drill down to lower levels of detail within the model. These drill-downs use the most current structures. When the lowest level of the business model is reached, drill-downs are capable of going back to the underlying data source.

The CPM systems also allow end users to produce their own, unrestricted (security permitting) analyses. These analyses include sorting, color-coding, charting, and ad hoc calculations. These analyses can be saved and recalled by users at a later date but will then feature the most current data.

These analytical capabilities are essential if users are to detect variances and their causes. With them, CPM systems prevent surprises. Users are always aware of current and potential exceptions and have time to evaluate alternative courses of action. These analytical capabilities also greatly reduce the time and effort the typical finance staff spends in supporting end-user queries.

SUMMARY

The architecture of an application is often hidden from end-user view, but it will have an impact on the maintenance of a CPM solution and the processes that can be supported effectively. It is not sufficient for CPM systems to have most of the features discussed because the benefits of one feature may not be fully realized unless it is accompanied by others. For example, the web by itself will not make a system easier to support unless it also is accompanied by a central database, full process support, and end-user analysis. It is only by taking all features together that make true CPM applications easier to set up, maintain, and able to cope with continuous planning, budgeting, forecasting, financial consolidation, management reporting, and analysis. For this reason, CPM systems that consist of older-type applications that have been linked together are likely to fail.

Chapter 6 highlights some successful CPM system designs and reviews some of the benefits organizations are obtaining. Chapter 9 provides guidelines for evaluating vendor solutions that deliver true CPM functionality.

Endnotes

1. Hackett Best Practices, *2002 Book of Numbers: Strategic Decision-Making* (2002), 4.
2. Ibid.
3. Robert Blumstein and Henry Morris, *Worldwide Financial/Business Performance Management Software Forecast and Analysis, 2002–2006*, Document no. 27346 (Framingham, MA: IDC, 2002), 13.
4. Raymond R. Panko, *What We Know About Spreadsheet Errors*, Research Paper, University of Hawaii, 2000, 3, from web site http://panko.cba.hawaii.edu/ssr/Mypapers/whatknow.htm.
5. Bill Hostmann and Kevin Strange, *Data Model Options That Support CPM Deployments*, Research Note DF-15-9618, Gartner, Inc., May 3, 2002, 2–4.

CHAPTER 6

Corporate Performance Management at Work

EARLY ADOPTER APPROACH

Early adopters of corporate performance management (CPM) are visionaries. They have turned against conventional approaches to planning, budgeting, and reporting in the belief that there is a better way to manage the implementation of strategy.

In most cases, these visionaries have established partnerships with computer software vendors to exploit that vendor's technology expertise and experience in delivering solutions to other organizations. These partnerships are mutually fruitful. The vendor is able to use the experience to create solutions that it can take to the market with references from a live user base. The client organization is able to share the costs of developing a solution using the latest technologies and sometimes can influence its functionality. Gartner found that the success of early adopters' systems often depended on the capabilities of their business intelligence (BI) solution vendors.[1]

Development of these early solutions always started with a pressing problem that needed to be solved. For most of these organizations, the most pressing problem was that their current budgetary planning and reporting systems did not meet their needs. They were fragmented, disconnected from strategy, and expensive to maintain in terms of both cost and effort.

Gartner notes that early adopters of CPM had two common themes when implementing their CPM solutions:

1. The implementation of a second wave of Balanced Scorecard that more closely tied together operational and transactional data
2. The integration of disparate applications and processes such as budgeting, forecasting, consolidation, and financial reporting[2]

The designs and implementations of all the early adopter systems covered in this book were led by chief financial officers and are used by senior executives and operational managers to run their companies. These systems were seen as strategic to the organization's ability to manage corporate performance; they were not seen as "just another software package for budgeting." While some of these systems are not yet fully operational CPM solutions covering all aspects of performance management, all have been designed to deliver broad and expanding CPM capabilities over time.

Today's CPM early adopters report a number of benefits. Many remark on dramatically reduced cycle times, allowing them to complete tasks they never would have attempted with their old systems. Others comment on how they are better able to use their time. Rather than spending it collecting data, looking for errors, and replicating information, they can use their time to analyze results and test scenarios. They marvel at the improved quality of their data, which in turn inspires confidence among managers about the decisions they make. Early adopters believe that they are now better able to respond to changing business and customer needs, which leads to competitive advantage and increased shareholder value.

San Diego Unified Port District: United States

The San Diego Unified Port District is a special government entity responsible for the harbor, airport, and public tidelands of San Diego, California. Like many organizations early on the path toward CPM, the Port identified budgeting as a pain point within the organization.

"For years, we handled the input and review of budget information via spreadsheets," says Bob Graves, budget administrator for the Port.[3] "Our staff assistant maintained a monstrous multiple megabyte spreadsheet that had almost everything in it, including entries for the entire chart of accounts. She would copy one worksheet for each of the 40 departments onto individual diskettes, then mail each of them out for input and review. As departments submitted revisions, we had the perennial problem of having multiple versions of the information. Then it took two weeks to publish the budget book once all the numbers and worksheets were final."

In 2000, the Port implemented the first phase of a new CPM system to help with budget preparation. The system's central database helped the Port eliminate the version control issues it had with traditional spreadsheets. In addition, it helped the Port dramatically decrease cycle time, which became a factor when a major reorganization happened in the middle of that year's budgeting cycle. The reorganization affected about 40 percent of the Port's departments. In addition, once the budget was re-created, the organization had to make cuts and resubmit the budget. "Management wanted new numbers the next day—and we were able to do it with the new system. What used to take a week could now be done in a day," reports Graves.

A surprising nonchallenge, says Graves, was that "we didn't have an acceptance problem from our users. They wanted 24–7 online access to data. They wanted one version of the data. They wanted to get rid of the spreadsheets. The new system was an easy sell."

Today, the web-based system has over 100 registered users. "Fifty to sixty of those actively use it as part of the budgeting and monitoring process. The others use it randomly to perform analyses. Managers and analysts can use it to look at the budget as it's evolving. They can also look at actuals over time to perform trend analysis. Soon we'll have eight years of actuals and nine years of budgets in the system," says Graves.

During the initial sales cycle, Graves says the Port did not fully understand all the benefits that the CPM solution could deliver. "The product had a lot more capability than we thought. We had to really think about what we wanted to use. It was good news/bad news." Today Graves reports that the Port has taken the system "way beyond our initial vision. For example, we really didn't understand the product's capability for online reporting, but now we're using it extensively. The managers are really happy about being able to access information online and about being able to look at the information in different ways. In the fall of 2002 we will create a control panel for our executives—a single dashboard where they can view critical information as soon as it's available, not just monthly."

The Port also has benefited from the system's ability to create alternative scenarios quickly, according to Graves. After the September 11,

2001, attacks, revenues dropped dramatically but expenses did not. In addition, some new legislation was proposed within a week of the terrorist attacks that would separate the airport from the rest of the district. Management wanted a revised revenue and expense budget for 2002 and new forecasts for 2003 that would reflect the bad economy with the airport remaining part of the district and a bad economy with the airport leaving the control of the district. "Plus they wanted a five-year cash flow forecast for all three scenarios. We had three days to do it—and we did it, with our new CPM system! We spent late nights to do it, but to this day, I'm amazed we could do it at all. We wouldn't have even tried it before," reports Graves.

Graves, who has several CPM projects scheduled through 2007, has a vision for how the Port will be able to use the system to enhance its ability to measure its strategic execution. "We have a conventional line-item budget right now. Next we plan to go to program-based budgeting," he reports. The Port's "programs" are actually strategies for the organization's five core areas of operation. "After that, we'll go to performance-based budgeting." Graves also says that the group is moving closer to implementing a Balanced Scorecard methodology that will help the organization in its efforts to better execute strategy.

Matáv: Hungary

Matáv is Hungary's largest telecommunications company with revenues of $1.6 billion. In 1998 the company was awarded the *Financial Times* Global Telecommunications Award as the most competitive national carrier. In 2002 it was awarded Euromoney's Award for Good Corporate Governance.

"Our original systems for planning, budgeting, consolidation, and reporting were very difficult to operate and manage, making it virtually impossible to model the business," says Zita Imrene Kartyik, head of business planning at Matáv.[4] "There was no common database in the company and its subsidiaries, making the financial data consolidation process difficult and leaving very little time for reporting and analysis. To meet our corporate goals, it was critical to find a solution that would help the planning team execute the strategic plan more effectively."

The new CPM solution combines all these processes into a single enterprise system that provides powerful functionality for tasks such as business modeling and "what if" analysis. The system follows a rolling three-year planning methodology. "Top-down targets for the group and its subsidiaries are set by the business planning division on the basis of market research and owners' and analysts' expectations. These are contrasted with bottom-up plans prepared by each business unit," explains Kartyik. "Both need to be aligned, so we go through a process of reallocation of targets and resources by either modifying the top-down target, adjusting unit targets to maintain the overall group target, or adjusting the group target."

The CPM solution has proven a major success with more than twice the number of users predicted in the original project plan. "Over 100 users including planners, financial controllers, analysts, and unit managers are using the solution," confirms Kartyik. "We can now quickly pinpoint deviations from strategy because actual and budget data are stored in one database. Management can therefore manage corporate performance more effectively."

ICI Paints: United Kingdom

ICI Paints, one of the world's largest manufacturers of paints and industrial coatings, recently experienced a rapid expansion of its United Kingdom (U.K.) operation that made rigorous budgeting in regard to performance management both more necessary and more difficult. The acquisition of the Cuprinol, Polycell, and Hammerite brands in 1998 introduced a new level of complexity into a business that was already coping with the challenge of multiple manufacturing sites and 120 retail outlets.

The first phase of the CPM solution concentrated on solving two problems: how to (1) reflect the multidimensional nature of the business and (2) streamline the growing budgeting process. "Most businesses still budget on two-dimensional spreadsheets, yet they operate in multiple dimensions, based on products, services, and customers. If the technology doesn't reflect that multidimensional reality, it's always going to fall short," says Martin Harrison, finance director—retail U.K. for ICI.[5]

"We were looking for a single system that provided one common version of the truth," Harrison notes. "We were also keen to put in a multicurrency system that could potentially be rolled out across Europe, and it had to be web-based because of the ease of rollout. We also wanted our users to view the true multidimensional nature of the data—to be able to see and understand our customer/product matrix, which is at the heart of understanding our business drivers." "Businesses that do not spend time understanding these issues and do not have the technology to capture this information will not be winners."

Another problem facing ICI Paints was "who owns the budget and performance data—the business unit manager or the category manager? The answer, of course, is both," says Harrison. "In the old process, each element of the U.K. business submitted a budget to Europe. Budgets were added together, which resulted in category figures that were not necessarily appropriate, and the process would start all over again. With the new CPM system, we now have a transparent system where both the national manager and the category manager can see the budget as it's built up. We've taken months out of our budgeting cycle."

The system's central database has proven to be a tremendous time saver because any changes made are reflected immediately throughout the system. "The system phases our budget automatically and links all the way through to our balance sheet and cash flow," says Harrison. "Processing changes is very easy because you know you are making all the appropriate changes on all three statements in every single period." Additionally, the company is taking advantage of the system's exception reporting capabilities. "With exception reporting, the system delivers the appropriate information at the appropriate time to managers who are not financially literate. We can get to detailed issues easily without clouding people with enormous amounts of data."

Implementing the CPM system has helped to deepen understanding among all employees of important business drivers. "We started to see how crude and inadequate some of our old budgeting was," says Harrison. "The system forced a new level of rigor and consistency across our organization. If you have all your measures in line, then you've got a fighting chance of doing true and value-adding external measurement of your performance."

Baker and Taylor: United States

Baker and Taylor is a leading supplier of books, movies, music, and information products to libraries and retailers worldwide. Like many other organizations, Baker and Taylor started its CPM implementation by focusing on the budgeting process. The data model allows planning by product, market, customer, sales, and functional areas, while the reporting and analysis model includes product, market, customer, shipping method, and geographic destination so that the organization can analyze cost of sales.

James Sharrett, the company's financial planning and systems manager at the time the system was designed, built the model without having complete specifications. He remembers, "There were a lot of unknowns, especially about how people did the budget. It's amazing how much people don't know about their budgeting process and what's in the general ledger."[6]

The benefits of the new CPM system today include business managers having a better understanding of the numbers, better communication of this information throughout the organization, and an increased focus on strategies to improve the bottom line. Interestingly, Baker and Taylor has found little change in the budgeting process cycle time. Instead, it has benefited from participation, accountability, and accuracy. "Before implementation of the CPM system, finance did 50 to 60 percent of the budget. It was very complicated with spreadsheets. About 10 people worked on the budget," says Brad Lucas, vice president of finance for Baker and Taylor.[7] "Now we are able to involve the business units (more than 40 people) in the process—the people who actually drive sales, expenses, and so on. The budgets are more accurate, which then leads to data that's more accurate. It snowballs—everything keeps getting better and better! It's all about accurate data and access."

Brisbane City Council: Australia

Brisbane City Council (BCC) is in the business of creating a better Brisbane, Australia. Its mission, by the year 2010, is to ensure that Brisbane is a prosperous city, enjoyed by residents, admired by visitors, and respected nationally and internationally for its achievements.

In 1999 BCC had two corporate performance management issues it wanted to address in support of this mission. First, this progressive organization was undertaking a fundamental review of its budgeting process for the headquarters and 12 departments and commercialized business units. The council wanted to move from a program-based accrual budget to a results-based accrual budget and meld together the strategic planning and budgeting processes.

As this reengineering was taking place, BCC also recognized a need to replace its homegrown budgeting system, which resided on a non-Y2K-compliant mainframe. This system was difficult to maintain and enhance, and provided inflexible budgeting and cumbersome reporting capabilities. The system was increasingly being augmented by the use of spreadsheets, which introduced security problems, version control issues, and maintenance woes.

According to Greg Ponych, principal finance officer—budget for BCC, "We wanted to better execute our strategic plan and reflect it in our operational plans. This required considerable effort, coordination, and management. We needed a system to make this process easier and more effective, one that could help us achieve our vision to make Brisbane the most livable and progressive city in the Asia-Pacific region."[8]

To unify its CPM processes and improve the reliability of its information, Brisbane City Council chose a technology solution with a centralized database. The single application was able to integrate planning, budgeting, and reporting. Additionally, it was one of the few web-based systems available at the time that could operate on the council's Oracle database. The system's openness was also a factor in the choice. According to council members, "Elements of our budget process reengineering were still evolving, and we needed to be sure that any future direction we wanted to pursue could be supported by our choice of a new technology system."

The council's budget analysts and strategic planners participated in the design of the system. Starting in December 1999, they began rolling out their application. The first phase addressed budgeting. The second phase addressed monitoring and analysis. The third encompassed strategic planning. Each phase took approximately three months to complete. Today the system is used by BCC's financial controllers, strategic planners, the chief financial and chief executive officers, and approximately 300 operational users.

"Our CPM system helps us attach the 'why' and 'how well' to the 'who,' 'what,' and 'by when,'" reports the Council, which improves strategic execution and organizational accountability. "We use a combination of Balanced Scorecard, triple bottom line [a measurement of the economic, environmental, and social value an organization creates or destroys], and key performance indicators to help us measure how well we have implemented our strategy—that is, how well the people of Brisbane accept the services we provide and the impact of providing these services. Many of our measures are nonfinancial."

With the unified database, BCC has been able to eliminate duplicate and triplicate versions of data and the problems associated with this occurrence. "We don't argue about the validity of the numbers anymore," according to the Council. Users are confident that the data are consistent and reliable. "With the single business model and web architecture, we're also able to keep pace with structure changes without having a truckload of programmers," members say. When the application is updated or information is added, the results are immediately available to the organization, ensuring that users always access the current application and data.

"Another benefit is the ability to analyze information and make recommendations instead of just reporting numbers," according to the Council. "Users are alerted to exceptions in the underlying data and can spend time analyzing significant business issues rather than spending that time wading through bulky reports. We're starting to look at trend information over longer periods of time, too, and we are beginning to get an idea of what the future might look like. Our users also have begun to see that they can look at overall performance, not just the financials."

While Brisbane City Council reports that there has been some reduction in process cycle time—saying "Corporate review of the budget prior to its presentation to the CEO has been reduced from three weeks to one week" and "We don't have people working on the budgets and reports until 2:00 A.M. anymore,"—members feel that the real value of CPM has been the reduced burden involved in budgeting and the value the organization is getting from its processes. "The quality of what we're doing is so much better," they report.

As anyone who has implemented an enterprise-wide system would predict, implementing corporate performance management was not without its challenges for BCC. According to Ponych, "I think the first two phases of the implementation were made more difficult because we were recreating our processes at the same time we were trying to build the technology system. I wouldn't recommend building a system until the business processes are finalized and clearly understood by everyone."

Ponych continues: "We actually ended up recreating our business model after the first two phases of the technology system were implemented. We just had too much detail. It's important to carefully consider what you're really going to need and what you're really going to use. Don't just repeat what you used to do. Also, I think it would have been helpful to spend more time up front looking at what we could do to make life easier for our various users. If we had engaged more users initially, I think they would have been more aware that we weren't just replacing systems because of Y2K. We wanted to take this as an opportunity to change what we were doing in order to make it better."

Brisbane City Council soon will begin its fourth CPM phase: detail project evaluation. This functionality will enable the council to improve its already robust project review and approval process through stronger data integration and by making the right information available at the right time of the process. This visionary organization also will be integrating more types of data into its CPM system in the quest to increase the efficiency and effectiveness of the performance management processes that support its vision of creating a better Brisbane.

Dutton-Forshaw: United Kingdom

Dutton-Forshaw is a leading European automotive and machinery group operating in a fiercely competitive, low-margin market. The group employs 1,800 people and has a yearly turnover of £450 million.

Following a management buyout from Lonrho in 1997, Dutton-Forshaw inherited a decentralized culture with 51 independent operating units. Competition was intense and the senior management team needed to control costs, improve margin opportunities, and culturally integrate the group for competitive advantage.

"Motor retailing is a low-margin, high-overhead business," says Charles Cameron, finance director, Dutton-Forshaw Group.[9] "Operating margins typically range between 1 percent and 3 percent. The manufacturers are keen to establish competitive advantage by ensuring brands are portrayed in modern environments utilizing the latest technology, which requires significant investment. Success depends on delivering excellence in customer service in a cost efficient manner.

"The growth in accounting and transaction systems in the business overwhelmed management with too much information and the relevance of the data was being lost. Without key performance management information, we were going to struggle," says Cameron. "We decided to build a single system on a central database that could support all aspects of the financial management process—planning, budgeting, forecasting, and management accounting—and provide strong online reporting to allow executives and managers greater access to key data."

In addition, the company traditionally had a decentralized culture that had each of the dealership units "reinventing the wheel." "The company suffered from silo management," says Cameron. "Everyone kept their own ideas and wouldn't learn off other people. We had to move towards a more open style of management culture within the business and break down these barriers." Dutton-Forshaw chose a CPM solution that enabled it to use its existing database technology, which would simplify the integration of data from its numerous internal systems.

"The CPM system has enabled us to reappraise the whole planning, budgeting, and reporting process," says Cameron. "Previously, we wasted time in games of financial tennis, producing thousands of numbers by site and division. Future planning and forecasting processes will be a lot more efficient. Using one version of the truth undoubtedly saves significant time." Divisional directors have access to the CPM system to drill down from the consolidated view to trial balance to examine individual dealership performance, uncover hidden details, and compare overheads between departments in similar or different franchises.

By implementing a CPM system, Dutton-Forshaw can now benchmark performance across business units, allowing managers to share best practices and improve sales performance. Cameron owned the implementation, and the project was finance oriented because the company's key metrics are largely financial.

"Dutton-Forshaw has achieved significant benefits and return on investment," says Cameron. "Some of the benefits are intangible, but they support broader strategic initiatives like the development of best practices and a learning corporate culture. As a result, management is much more focused on key issues and this has increased their ability to respond quickly to changing market conditions.

"With the CPM system, users can compare their unit overheads and profit margins with units in similar or different franchises. Two Land Rover dealerships may have the same throughput but widely differing expense bases. With CPM users can immediately see the relevant information," explains Cameron.

"Being able to compare information, whether it's year on year, budget or forecast, and being able to do it quickly with exception reporting is a major advantage," says Cameron. "It is very easy to look at the trends within expenses and identify where, at a divisional or a unit level, we have a particular problem. It also allows us to benchmark activities that we weren't able to do before. The CPM system is a very powerful application and undoubtedly this is having a direct benefit on the business.

"The CPM system also highlights if there is a problem beneath a consolidated number," says Cameron. "For example, the profitability for Dovercourt Ford may be better than the previous year, but the system highlights any underlying problems. I can drill down to the unit, identify the problem, and send an e-mail to the manager or director to ask them what action they are going to take."

As an expanding company, Dutton-Forshaw also recognized it needed a management system that would be flexible as the company acquired new dealerships and operating units. "Dutton-Forshaw is an evolving company, and the business structure continually changes. Adding and removing units and associated data is easy with the CPM solution," states Cameron. "It has helped us to develop the business and manage it in the way we want to be going forward. We look forward to continuing our strong relationship with the CPM software vendor, leveraging their product and experience, and developing the application further to ensure Dutton-Forshaw remains a leading distributor and retailer."

Advantage Sales & Marketing: United States

"Before we implemented a corporate performance management system, the CEO had to act on consensus and gut feeling. Now he can slice and dice daily information to base his decisions on. It's the difference between flying by sight versus flying by radar," says Bob Vesely, executive vice president and CFO of Advantage Sales & Marketing LLC.[10]

Advantage is a member-owned brokerage company that provides global sales, marketing, and retail services to the consumer packaged goods industry, supporting its clients' worldwide distribution channels. The company serves client food and nonfood manufacturers by supporting thousands of the items consumers see on shelves in their local grocery, mass, drug, club, and convenience stores. The organization's mission is to be the most efficient and effective sales and marketing company in every market in which it operates.

When the company had only seven divisions and 50 departments, spreadsheet budgeting and reporting worked adequately as a corporate performance management tool, according to Vesely. In 1999, however, anticipating the company's growth to today's 100 divisions, hundreds of departments, and 12,500 associates, Vesely saw the need to improve the information flow between the company's offices and hundreds of managers. "We knew that we were rapidly moving to a national reporting platform, and we wanted a web-based budgeting and reporting application with multidimensionality. We wanted to empower decision makers with the most current information and analysis capabilities, and we needed to create accountability for the budgeting process at the department manager level," recalls Vesely.

Vesely spearheaded the specification and design of his organization's CPM system. He included input from sales and finance professionals. "I wanted Sales to own it," he says, so gaining their understanding, support, and contributions early in the process was important. The business model included typical structures such as customer, client, geographical region, and others. "Advantage is a service company, so we measure revenue by services. We look at data by year, quarter, and month. We generally don't review revenue data more frequently than monthly because our clients generally use a monthly basis of measurement." Additionally, the technology solution would need to integrate with the company's Microsoft database, its enterprise information portal (TriNet), and a variety of data sources.

The first phase of the system was rolled out to financial personnel in 2000. Data were integrated into the system nightly from the organization's multiple member accounting systems. Functionality of the new system encompassed the creation of income statements, balance sheets, and cash flow statements as well as calculation of ratios, automated allocations, and the ability to perform multidimensional analysis. Vesely estimates that it took approximately 90 days to implement and cost $250,000. Fifty percent of the cost was the investment in hardware and software, while the other 50 percent was accounted for in terms of the time spent by developers, programmers, and internal resources, including the company's full-time system administrator.

Looking back on the initial implementation, Vesely identifies two areas he would do differently if he were starting over today. "I wouldn't create as many reports. We duplicated a number of existing accounting reports to make people comfortable with the new system. I think that kept people from really exploring the full functionality of this powerful multidimensional system. Also, I think we could have developed more training tools to help our users. What we did was adequate, but we could have done more."

Phase 1 of the CPM system was quickly followed by phase 2, which added sales management functionality to the system. Data were integrated nightly from the enterprise's order management system databases. Now in addition to the finance staff, management and sales personnel access the system directly and easily evaluate data that previously was available only in hard-copy reports (see Exhibits 6.1 through 6.3). "Today 500 people use the system, 30 percent of whom are frequent users of the system and 70 percent of whom visit the system periodically," reports Vesely.

Phase 3 started in 2002 and involves three aspects. The first is the expansion of data exported from the order management system and other data silos to develop an executive information system (EIS) on the web. "We want to push our CPM solution to new levels by adding additional

Exhibit 6.1   Advantage Sales & Marketing creates a strategic plan, divides it into short- and long-term initiatives, and allocates resources to them. System users can monitor plan progress and results.

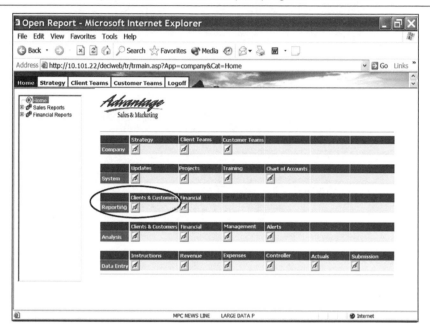

management-based data that was only available from persons managing various applications," states Vesely. Second is the effort to formally integrate the strategic planning process into the EIS reporting system, budgeting process, and performance management process. Vesely says, "This is a longer process that will continue to expand the ease of access by management to data that is critical to day-to-day decision making." The final aspect is expanded web-based training and e-training. "Our team is making great progress on training at the web with streaming video. This is critical as we continue to expand the user base throughout the company," reports Vesely.

Vesely says, "Our ability to easily access the system and use it to slice and dice revenue by client and by customer on any desktop in the world is a huge advantage. The web makes it so easy and cheap to provide consistent communication and measure performance across our organization."

While the organization has benefited from small improvements in process speeds, Vesely says, "The real difference is the value of the time

Exhibit 6.2   A user clicks on a link to see the sales tactics by strategic client.

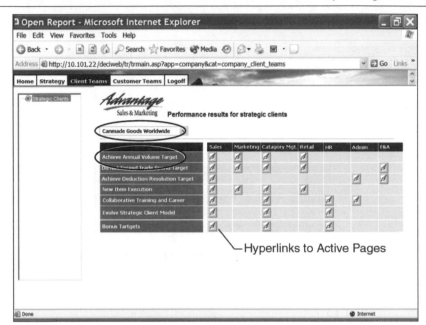

we're spending. A faster budgeting process is great, but the real benefit is if it's right when you get it. Our processes have been enhanced. Instead of spending our time doing data entry and checking for errors, we're getting our results quicker and spending more time analyzing the results."

Vesely believes that management's commitment to the strategic planning process is key to the plan's successful execution and evolution. Everyone has a role to play. The CFO's role, in his experience, is to drive the design and implementation of a system that enables strategic execution and to provide performance management and oversight.

Soon the organization expects to see the benefits of the final phase. It will encompass the daily integration of retail reporting, the ability to perform detail planning for payroll, and add activity-based costing analysis, all of which will be linked to the corporate strategy. Ultimately 1,500 people are expected to use Advantage's system for corporate performance management as the organization continues to maintain its leadership in the marketplace through its process of continuous improvement.

Exhibit 6.3 The user sees the tactic, goal, goal owner, and deadline, and can click a link to view reports.

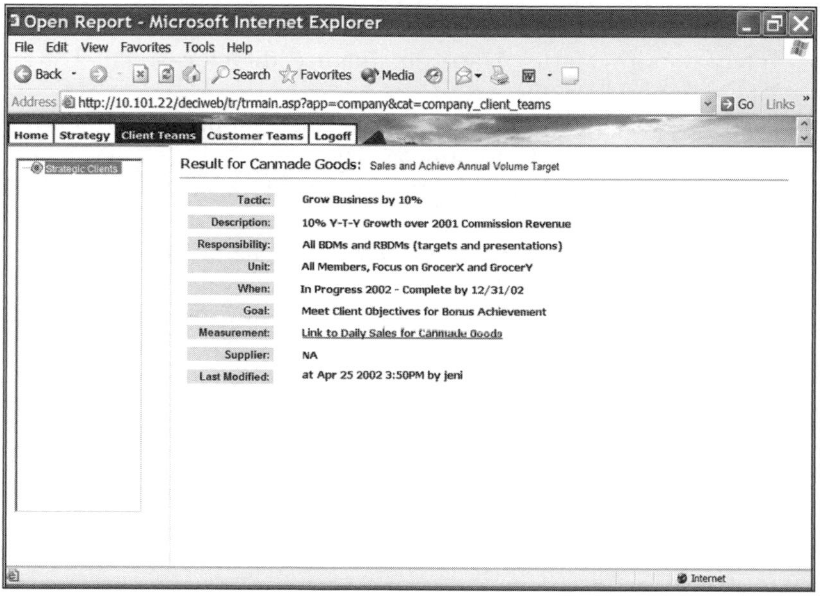

SUMMARY

Even in these early days of implementation, it is obvious that visionary organizations are reaping the benefits that CPM systems deliver. From improving the quality of—and access to—data; to enhancing the usefulness, timeliness, and value of information; to acquiring the ability to link strategy to resources, action, and reports, these early adopters are well on the way to improving their ability to eliminate the strategy gap within their organizations. Based on the experience of these and more than 100 other early adopters, the following chapters outline how organizations can start designing and implementing their own CPM systems.

Endnotes

1. Nigel Rayner, *Corporate Performance Management Benefits Early Adopters,* Research Note COM-15-9802, Gartner, Inc., May 3, 2002, 3.
2. Ibid., 1.

3. Interview with Bob Graves, budget administrator, San Diego Unified Port District, August 9, 2002.

4. Interview with Zita Imrene Kartyik, head of business planning, Matáv, August 13, 2002.

5. Interview with Martin Harrison, finance director—retail U.K., ICI Paints, August 7, 2002.

6. Interview with James Sharrett, former financial planning and systems manager, Baker and Taylor, July 25, 2002.

7. Interview with Brad Lucas, vice president of finance, Baker and Taylor, July 17, 2002.

8. Interview with Greg Ponych, principal finance officer—budget, Brisbane City Council, July 22, 2002.

9. Interview with Charles Cameron, finance director, Dutton-Forshaw Group, August 12, 2002.

10. Interview with Bob Vesely, executive vice president and CFO, Advantage Sales & Marketing, July 18, 2002.

CHAPTER 7

Getting Started

ONE PIECE AT A TIME

It is impractical and undesirable for an organization to attempt moving to a full-fledged corporate performance management (CPM) solution overnight. To begin with, these projects span the enterprise. As such, they involve higher costs, require more sophisticated levels of business and technical expertise, and have a greater risk of failure than more narrowly focused projects. The rewards, however, are potentially much greater. In approaching a CPM strategy, senior management must think of the implementation as not just a change in technology but as an opportunity to transform key business processes and improve managerial decision making in support of implementing strategy.

For this objective to be realized, any CPM implementation must be placed in the proper context. If the approach is to simply buy and install new software, then the result will simply be new software. Companies often assume that new technology will translate automatically into doing business "better, faster, smarter." But if the underlying business processes are flawed, "faster" will likely be the only achievement. Doing the wrong thing in 30 percent less time is hardly a benefit. In contrast, CPM implementations focus on effectively transforming strategy into action by combining methodologies and the right measures, presented to users as an ongoing, event-based process, supported by technology systems.

Gartner warns against trying to create an "ultimate" CPM strategy. Attempting to do so quickly becomes a theoretical exercise in which the organization tries to define every metric, process, and methodology that the enterprise will ever need. This approach is doomed to fail.[1] What organizations should do is carefully think through a road map that will allow a more strategic approach to deploying CPM. Suggestions for the elements of such a map are provided later in this chapter. Before beginning, however, assemble the team that will be responsible for guiding the CPM initiative.

CHOOSING THE RIGHT TEAM

A CPM solution yields true value to an organization only when it is placed in the service of achieving business objectives. Therefore, people within the organization who can identify these objectives—senior business managers—must be the system drivers. Because the formulation and implementation of strategy is one of the key responsibilities of the chief financial officer (CFO) and chief executive officer (CEO), they also must be part of the team. Active participation of senior management has been a key factor in the success of early adopters of CPM solutions.

Within the CPM implementation team, some clearly identifiable roles exist. These roles include CPM champion, technology advocate, and process management advocate. Other roles and personnel may be identified as being essential members of the team, but the roles mentioned here are key. Selecting the right people to fill these is critical to the CPM solution's success.

CPM Champion

The CPM champion is typically the organization's senior executive or one placed as highly within the organization as possible. The broad nature of change required by CPM, the major investment in financial and human resources that is necessary, and the importance of the project to the long-term success of the organization all call for the active sponsorship, support, and leadership of the senior business executive. Because the impetus for implementing a performance management solution is to gain a competitive business advantage, it should be treated as a business initiative, not an information technology (IT) project. Therefore, a business executive, not an IT manager or information officer, must champion the process.

The champion must be able to express the big picture, communicating the value and importance of the project throughout the entire organization. Besides acting as an advocate, the champion also will need to be a diplomat. An enterprise-wide solution touches on many areas, making it inevitable that interdepartmental or jurisdictional disputes will arise. The champion must know enough about both the finance and IT functions to mediate disputes when they arise.

The champion also must be prepared to stay committed and active throughout the entire length of the CPM initiative and beyond. Dennis Ganster, CEO of Comshare, believes that CPM is more than a project: It's a way of life. "CPM systems need to be continually used and updated. It they aren't, they grow stale or die," says Ganster. "The CEO's role in pushing a CPM system forward and making sure people update and use it is vital if the organization is to successfully execute its strategy." Others in the organization will take their cue from the champion. If the champion appears to lose interest and CPM is not seen as the priority, they will assume that the project has been devalued and act accordingly.

Technology Advocate

Corporate performance management systems are complex in that they provide a single view of performance to the whole organization. The technology infrastructure of an organization cannot be changed easily, and any change can have a high cost in terms of financial investment and operating efficiency. For this reason, the CPM project team must include a technology advocate who understands the current and planned IT direction for the organization and who can advise on what may or may not be possible, practical, and desirable.

To provide a single view of the organization, the IT advocate will need to understand how to use the CPM solution to integrate data from the organization's core internal systems and from a variety of external information sources. The advocate will need to ensure that the CPM solution makes data accessible to organizational members around the enterprise in a format that is usable and adheres to the existing communications protocols. Similarly, if an organization is undergoing change to a new technology infrastructure, the IT advocate must ensure that the CPM solution can adapt to the organization's existing—or future—IT infrastructure. Imagine finding yourself, for example, with a general ledger system that no longer works because of some technology change. The IT advocate ensures that the system will operate from a technology point of view.

Process Management Advocate

The organization's processes for planning, budgeting, forecasting, and reporting are the main point of contact for managers and budget holders when implementing and monitoring strategy. The processes must function effectively. Therefore, a member of the finance department usually is named as the process management advocate. This advocate must be involved in the design of any new or modified processes and in putting processes into action as the CPM system is delivered.

As a relatively new concept, CPM can easily be mistaken for an extension of existing systems. It is different in that it is a strategy, not just a technology solution. Team members who guide the CPM initiative must be aware of that difference and how it impacts the organization. Having the team read this book can enhance the education process. Some successful early adopters have held workshops, led by external CPM consultants, for their executives and managers. The result of these workshops is a common understanding of what can be accomplished and a jump-start on building a CPM road map for the organization.

BUILDING A CPM ROAD MAP

Solutions are best built through small, or "phased," implementations that initially address key business "pain points." However, these pain points must be addressed in the context of a long-term CPM road map that identifies how any short-term initiatives fit into the overall strategy.[2] Doing so will mean that benefits realized early in the project will provide the impetus for successive implementations. From experience gathered working with early adopters, Comshare has developed 10 steps for building a CPM road map.

Define Key Performance Metrics

Gartner states that the formulation of strategy should be the driving force in designing a CPM solution.[3] Before committing large expenditures of time and money, organizations should review their goals and objectives at the highest level. Next, they should clearly define their key performance indicators and how they are to be achieved. This is in essence what strategic planning is all about: ensuring that the right performance data are planned and monitored by the right people within the organization at an appropriate level of detail.

Define Methodologies to Support Metrics

Once the key metrics have been identified, the method of delivering them needs to be determined. For many CPM applications, this methodology takes the form of a "scorecard" that ensures all aspects of the organization are covered (see Exhibit 7.1). Kaplan and Norton's Balanced Scorecard helps organizations ensure that their strategy covers both short- and long-term performance. It focuses attention on the different aspects that impact viability: financial results, operational efficiency, customers, and learning and growth. Even if the methodology is not adhered to exactly, it does provide a good way to break down corporate objectives into divisional and departmental plans.

Detailed elements of the scorecard can be based around activities, such as is done with activity-based management (ABM), or on the value each asset adds, such as is done using the Economic Value Added (EVA) methodology. Although these are different techniques, they still focus on the achievement of corporate goals whose results can be displayed as a scorecard. The point of this activity is to agree, at a high level, to the way in which performance will be managed throughout the organization.

Define CPM Processes

This step is a high-level review of how the CPM processes should work in planning and monitoring the organization's goals and objectives. This review should answer questions relative to each of the processes outlined in Chapter 3:

- Who will be involved?
- What level of detail will be employed during the process?
- What event will trigger each process?

This review also should answer:

- How will the strategy be formulated? This question addresses how particular strategies will be assessed and chosen and the way in which the resulting top-down targets will be established.
- How will tactical plans be created and funded? This covers the interaction between budget holders and management in developing tactical plans aligned to strategy, the way in which resources will be allocated to those plans, and how management should review the resulting budget.

Exhibit 7.1 Scorecard showing how strategy and tactics affect organizational departments.

Financial Strategies
Maintain Profitable Growth

Tactic	Sales	Marketing	Production	F&A	HR
Total revenues in line with market growth	○		○		○
Control overall expenditure growth	○	○			
Reduce general & admin. expenses	○	○	○		○
Keep overall salary raises to 5%	○	○	○	○	○
Improve sales productivity	○			○	

Customer Strategies
Achieve 95% Customer Satisfaction

Tactic	Sales	Marketing	Production	F&A	HR
Open new international call center		○		○	○

Improve Customer Loyalty

Tactic	Sales	Marketing	Production	F&A	HR
Launch quarterly customer magazine	○	○	○		
Trade-in scheme for older products	○	○			

Internal Strategies
Improve Product Quality

Tactic	Sales	Marketing	Production	F&A	HR
Invest in latest automated production equipment			○		○
Increase quality assurance staffing			○		○

Improve Sales Lead Generation

Tactic	Sales	Marketing	Production	F&A	HR
Create new website for eCommerce		○		○	

Development Strategies
Retain the Best People

Tactic	Sales	Marketing	Production	F&A	HR
Reward all employees with annual bonus	○	○	○	○	○
Maintain full number of sales reps				○	○

Recruit Management Internally

Tactic	Sales	Marketing	Production	F&A	HR
Specialized training for all staff	○	○	○		

- How will plans be communicated? This covers the way plans appear to users and the events that will be used to change organizational behavior.
- How will plans be monitored? The question addresses the process for identifying, communicating, and acting on actual exceptions to the plan.
- How will forecasts be handled? The organization needs to determine how far out it should forecast, and establish a process for identifying, communicating, and dealing with forecasted exceptions.
- How will information be reported? This covers the generation and communication of results to internal and external stakeholders.

The review will result in a document containing the work flow of data through the various processes. It serves to enhance management's understanding of the way in which CPM could work within the organization (see Exhibit 7.2). A sample form for this work is included in Appendix A.

Exhibit 7.2   High-level review of a proposed CPM process for budgeting.

CPM Process: Creation and Funding of Tactical Plans

Activities:	Set goals	Issue instructions	Complete sales budget	Complete expenses budget	Conduct budget review	Review written plans	Issue capital budget
Level of Detail:	Total sales by product Total expense by activity		Sales by marketing initiative	Expense by activity	By activity By product	By activity	By project cash flow
People Involved:	Senior mgmt.	Budget admin.	Sales divisions	Marketing	Divisional heads	Senior mgmt.	Finance dept.
Triggered by:	>10% varience from plan	Board agreement on new goals	Receipt of new goals	Receipt of sales targets	5 days from issuing new goals	2 days following review	2 days following review

Overlay Existing Processes

On this review document, management next must compare what actually happens versus what it said should happen (see Exhibit 7.3). It needs to focus on the ways in which processes are triggered, the type of data that flows, and the users involved. It is surprising how many organizations do not really understand the processes that are actually in place, but such understanding is necessary if those processes are to be changed.

Identify Strategic Gaps

After comparing the ideal CPM process to what actually happens, organizations will be able to identify a number of gaps in current processes that prevent the effective communication and monitoring of strategy. Answering the next questions also can help reveal many of these gaps:

- Does the strategic plan adequately cover all aspects of the organization? If not, what areas are missing?

Exhibit 7.3 What actually happens during the budgeting process.

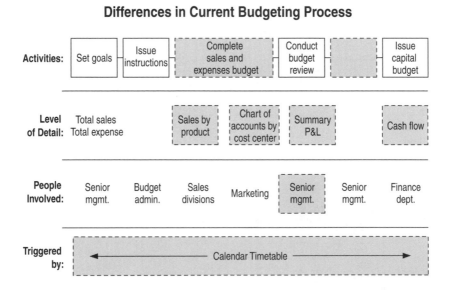

Differences in Current Budgeting Process

Activities:	Set goals	Issue instructions	Complete sales and expenses budget	Conduct budget review	Issue capital budget
Level of Detail:	Total sales / Total expense		Sales by product	Chart of accounts by cost center / Summary P&L	Cash flow
People Involved:	Senior mgmt.	Budget admin.	Sales divisions	Marketing / Senior mgmt.	Senior mgmt. / Finance dept.
Triggered by:			Calendar Timetable		

146

- What processes are missing or are inadequately covered?
- Are the market assumptions, including economic and competitor assumptions, recorded and monitored throughout each process?
- Can the defined metrics that appear in the strategic plan be monitored through each part of the CPM process? In what parts of the process do they fail to appear?
- Do the detailed written tactical plans tie in to the corporate strategy? Can they be measured and monitored throughout all the CPM processes?
- Can the planned, actual, and forecasted progress of strategic initiatives be tracked individually?
- What information is not getting to the right people?
- What information is being distributed that is superfluous to the implementation of strategy?
- What feedback loops or triggers that start a process are missing?
- What detailed analysis behind summary numbers is missing?

The answers to these questions should be documented, and the organization should determine whether the gap is being caused by the systems being used, the methodology being adopted, or simply a failure to consider something important when the system was implemented.

Identify Pain Points

The next step in building a CPM road map is to identify the pains being experienced in the current processes and the causes of those pains. The budgeting and forecasting process is the most likely source of pain in organizations.[4] Many organizations still rely on spreadsheets and lengthy budgeting processes that do not respond easily to change or to the needs of management.

When identifying pain points, it is vital that the organization expose the root causes of the pain or issues that need to be corrected. For example, if the budgeting process takes too long, what are the contributing factors? Does it take too long because budget holders are submitting their budgets late? Is it because the budget submissions are incomplete or not within the established guidelines? Perhaps it is because the managers do not understand this once-a-year process or the system being used is too complex for novices.

Assess Planned Business Intelligence Initiatives

At any given time, an organization may be planning or implementing various business intelligence initiatives. It is important to review these initiatives because a particular one could work against the implementation of a CPM solution. For example, if a new customer relationship management (CRM) analysis system is being implemented, it is important to know whether it can form part of a detailed store beneath the reporting of a summary CRM measure. If the CRM analysis system is a stand-alone solution, then it may be difficult or impossible to integrate it into the final CPM system. This would result in having two systems that could cause integrity problems because each system could potentially give different results. It also would double the maintenance effort because there would be two models to maintain.

Corporate performance management solutions are built on top of a business intelligence (BI) platform that could and should be used for as many BI initiatives as possible. In this way, administrators have only one set of technologies to learn, and integration between the various data stores will be greatly simplified. Reviewing all the current and planned BI initiatives may help to leverage development effort and will certainly help in the planning of any integration that may be required in the future.

Calculate Return on Investment

The return on investment of a CPM system should be assessed relative to the strategic gaps and pain points being resolved. Because systems are expensive and resources are limited, organizations have to continually assess whether any effort is worthwhile. Without calculating return on investment (ROI) and quantifying value, it is too easy for organizations to cancel or delay essential initiatives. In addition to helping convey the value of a CPM implementation, calculating ROI also helps enterprises set priorities and choose the order in which initiatives are implemented. The calculation of ROI is discussed in detail later in this chapter.

Set Implementation Priorities

Having established the value of delivering the various components of a CPM solution, the order in which to implement them can be determined. The best way to do this is to consider five aspects of the existing system(s) and how it needs to change over time:

1. *Comprehensive.* Does the system cover all aspects of the organization (sales, production, materials, labor, overhead, capital, cash, etc.), leading and lagging indicators, and intangibles?
2. *Strategic.* How strategic is the system in terms of sharing the corporate vision, linking initiatives to operating budgets, and focusing on objectives that drive the organization forward?
3. *Analytical.* How analytical is the system in terms of analyzing key performance indicators, highlighting the status of strategy, providing alerts on exceptions, and allowing user-driven ad hoc investigations?
4. *Collaborative.* Does the system allow the alignment of data and targets across different levels of the organization? Does it provide feedback loops and support end-user scenario planning?
5. *Effectiveness.* How efficient is the system in terms of the length of time it takes to perform a process? How automated is it? Does it provide automated exception alerts?

Each of these aspects can be plotted as axes on a radar chart, with the innermost point representing little or no achievement and the outermost point representing the ideal situation (see Exhibit 7.4). These charts are based on perceptions and may vary between user communities, but they do provide a framework from which to assess and agree on priorities.

Exhibit 7.4   The state of a current solution for CPM.

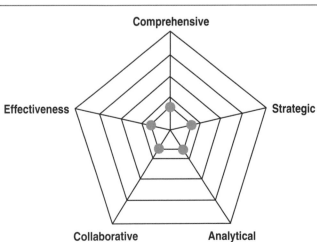

Organizations should use the CPM solution to solve the most critical business pains first. If users have to wait six months before they see any changes or improvements, the initiative is likely to fail due to loss of interest or a change in priority. Many organizations feel that their major pain point is the length of time it takes to budget. Therefore, they focus on budgeting effectiveness and efficiency first. This initiative becomes phase 1 of their CPM implementation. Once this has been implemented, other pain points are addressed until they are all at the optimum level (see Exhibit 7.5).

Exhibit 7.5 The focus of phase 1 CPM implementation and beyond.

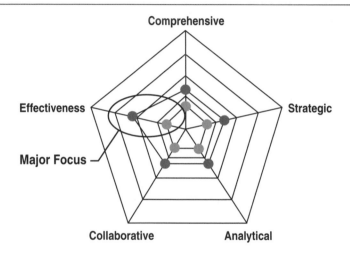

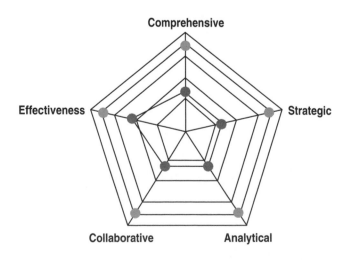

This phased approach to implementation provides four benefits.

1. The operation can solve its most painful problems first.
2. The organization can see the improvement quickly, generating interest and excitement.
3. Phasing allows users to get comfortable with the application a little at a time, which avoids overwhelming them and causing frustration.
4. Because users are comfortable, the system can be updated over time with additional functionality, with little trauma to the organization and reduced IT support requirements.

Amazon.com provides a good example of a phased implementation. This well-known online retailer started out by selling books using a straightforward web interface. Today Amazon's web site is an extremely sophisticated portal that learns about users' interests and preferences and can suggest and supply them with a wide range of goods. Amazon has achieved this sophistication through a series of continuous improvements that were barely detectable by regular users. Bit by bit, the system evolved to meet changing business needs. If Amazon had tried to implement all this functionality at once, it likely would have failed to achieve its current level of success because competitors would have stolen the marketplace. Similar to the development of Amazon's retail site, regular delivery of components that solve business issues and deliver superior ROI is a successful strategy in the deployment of CPM.

Reviewing the Road Map and Moving toward Implementation

The creation of a CPM road map is just the start. Once the organization identifies its priorities, it needs to specify and select a solution that can deliver the necessary benefits. It must create a project plan to deliver the solution. Chapter 8 covers the detailed design of a CPM solution, while Chapter 9 looks at the implementation of a solution.

Because business needs, priorities, and circumstances change over time—often frequently—and because the implementation of a particular initiative may reveal additional costs, organizations must revisit the CPM road map on a regular basis and ensure that it reflects the latest situation. The best time to do this is after a review on the impact of a particular development that has just been implemented.

CALCULATING RETURN ON INVESTMENT

Why Calculate Return on Investment?

Return on investment is a traditional evaluation method deployed by organizations to weigh the merits of undertaking new investments or projects. During the dot-com 1990s, it was more theory than practice. With the stock market in the midst of a record bull run, it seemed that the biggest return needed was an emotional one. All executives had to say was "It's all about e-commerce" or any other web-based technology, and the markets rewarded them handsomely. Unfortunately—or fortunately, for the fiscally responsible—it is no longer all about "e." It is all about how you use "e," and, more important, it is all about the payback. Like any business initiative, CPM projects need to be justified in terms of increasing shareholder value and profits or some other value proposition expected by the organization.

So how do companies evaluate ROI? When asked in a survey how they measure ROI on IT projects or IT spending, 150 respondents revealed a variety of measures (see Exhibit 7.6).

Looking at the list of responses, efficiency (decreased costs, increased productivity, reduced head count) and effectiveness (increased revenue) stand out as the two biggest issues in determining ROI. The remainder of this discussion focuses on some of the specific sources of efficiency and effectiveness within CPM systems and how organizations assign value in determining the expected returns.

Efficiency Gains from CPM Systems

Efficiency gains are the first place to look when analyzing returns from technology investments. Easy to understand and generally easier to estimate than other types of gains, solid returns from process improvements are a minimum requirement. While not necessarily covering the entire return picture, efficiency gains often are referred to as hard benefits in an ROI analysis. At a minimum, a CPM system should provide reduced cycle time, improved report development and distribution, improved analytic capabilities, improved financial consolidation, and the ability to close the books faster.

Reduced Cycle Time. Prior to implementing management systems, most companies rely on spreadsheets for the dissemination of budget templates and the subsequent data collection and consolidation. With these

152

Exhibit 7.6 How organizations say they measure ROI.

Determining ROI

Measure	% of Respondents
Decreased costs	83%
Length of time to payback	75%
Increased revenue	71%
Increase in productivity	70%
Project is up and running within a certain time	67%
Reduced head count	57%
Discounted cash flow	32%
Specific ROI formula or benchmark	19%
Not measuring ROI in IT projects	6%

Source: Gary H. Anthes, "Measuring Up,"
Computerworld, December 10, 2001. Reprinted with
permission of *Computerworld.*

spreadsheets comes a considerable investment in time: time creating models that reflect the organization's operations; time customizing budget templates for individual departments and functional areas; time creating consolidation links among the various templates; and so on. With a CPM system, the model is created once with common business rules, using a single, centralized database. This saves significant time. Using web technologies to access the models, organizations no longer need to distribute separate templates for each of the hundreds or thousands of budget holders throughout the enterprise. A single URL is distributed, and the system displays the applicable accounts to the budget holder as determined by the organizational hierarchy, functional responsibility, or any other criteria important to the organization. Manual processes that used to take days now take minutes. Additional time is saved through the elimination of complex linkages between spreadsheets and time-consuming, error-prone data transfers that are characteristic of earlier technology solutions (spreadsheet applications as well as more recent client/server budgeting applications).

Many organizations spend over half of their time performing manual processes. By automating these processes, enterprises can free up valuable finance resources from non–value-adding administrative tasks and apply them toward endeavors that are more strategic to the business. As they spend more time performing analyses and creating business plans with process owners, finance staff members become true business partners within the organization rather than remaining guardians of the numbers.

Improved Report Development and Distribution. Once the budget is completed, the next hurdle is reporting against the information. Traditionally, reporting has involved multiple applications spanning numerous legacy databases and outdated packaged applications. Corporate performance management systems solve this problem. Integrated with the application's central database, a CPM system has powerful reporting capabilities that are much easier to use and maintain than those of older, separate applications. Much attention has been paid to providing vast libraries of "standard" report structures and to creating user-friendly report design tools that enable non-IT practitioners to support almost all of the special reporting needs of the organization.

Distribution technology also is well developed in these solutions. Since CPM systems are capable of creating and distributing electronic report packs, human resources are no longer required to supervise manual report batch runs and the subsequent distribution of these reports across the organization in the next day's mail. In fact, depending on the user's inclination and the nature of the information, most reporting can move to real time thanks to the centralized database and web access inherent in a CPM solution.

In total, the savings from these powerful reporting functions can run into the tens if not hundreds of thousands of dollars, depending on the organization's size. Personnel costs can be reduced dramatically, information can be distributed immediately instead of on a weekly basis, and something as simple as the cost of paper saved can add up quickly.

Improved Analytic Capabilities. Instead of generating multiple reports across a variety of systems and then setting people loose to wander through the data, CPM systems deploy state-of-the-art alerting technologies and analytics to quickly focus people on the real opportunities and problems that reside in their organization's data. Corporate performance management systems are deployed on top of powerful databases that allow a business to be examined from numerous perspectives. Coupling these multiple perspectives with powerful charting and graphing capabilities provides unique insight into specific opportunities or problems. Users can then drill down to the underlying causes to better exploit opportunities and correct problems as appropriate.

The obvious hard benefit realized from improved analytics is the time saved researching issues. No longer must hundreds of managers and front-line decision makers pore over results only to confirm that everything is okay or, worse yet, to miss a subtle opportunity or looming problem. Instead, users are alerted directly to the important issues impacting their decisions.

The use of defined reporting and analysis methodologies has benefits beyond saving time; it also helps improve decision making. Issues as diverse as inventory control, contract renewals, and production planning all benefit from the more focused analytic capabilities of these new corporate performance management systems.

Improved Consolidation Process. With support for multiple hierarchies and more powerful consolidation engines, CPM systems reduce the work involved with periodic consolidation. Organizations reap immediate benefits because they eliminate the need for data transfers, manual reconciliations, quality control checks across multiple applications, distribution of templates, and maintenance of multiple databases as required by legacy and packaged applications.

Closing the Books Faster. Speed is another benefit delivered by CPM systems. Closing the books faster is easy to quantify in terms of time saved. It may seem difficult, however, to quantify seemingly intangible or "soft" benefits in more tangible terms. With some creativity, however, doing this is possible. For example, when a consultant asked a CFO of a multibillion-dollar company how much money his company could save by closing the books faster each month, no answer was forthcoming. Yet when the consultant asked the CFO's sales managers how much they could save if they did not hire extra personnel based on out-of-date sales forecast data, the answer was $1 million over five years.[5]

This is a powerful example. The hidden return was revealed only after understanding how people who received the closing numbers used them to make decisions. The impact of the decisions in this example equated to $1 million. This is just one example. Think about the variety of contracts based on volume that an organization negotiates regularly (monthly, quarterly, semiannually, or annually) throughout the year. Consider how great the impact would be if management knew enough to purchase 10 percent less for the period or could avoid a premium charge in scrambling for 10 percent more of whatever resource was under negotiation.

As another example, consider the positive impact of timely data and reports on the supply chain. Real-time data from a CPM system can highlight unfavorable trends as soon as they begin to occur, enabling the purchasing team to modify its decisions and actions immediately. If, however, the purchasing team must wait 30 to 90 days to see forecasts and sales trends, the team will base purchasing decisions on outdated information. When the trend is finally recognized, purchasing will likely underorder or overorder product. A smooth supply chain now will be plagued with aggravating spikes and valleys. Although it might not ever be evident explicitly on the invoice, purchasing departments with an inconsistent and erratic order history do not receive the best price. Someone has to pay for a supplier's rush orders and excess reserve stock. In this case that someone is the purchasing department that causes them. To realize the value of this benefit, a purchasing department can work on negotiating better terms in return for better forecasts. The larger the volume with the supplier in question, the larger the savings. The key is that a company must deliver better forecasts, which cannot be done with monthly numbers delivered three weeks after closing.

Effectiveness Gains with CPM Systems

After all the analysis has been done around reduced cycle times, cost of ownership, ease of use, and other factors, one confronts the real reason for moving toward a CPM system: competitive advantage. In today's economy, there is considerable pressure to focus on the tried and true and to go with the sure thing. A familiar approach might sound like this: "I won't approve anything with a payback period greater than 18 months or an ROI of less than 30 percent." Such an approach might work for catch-up or maintenance investments, but it never gave anyone a competitive advantage in the marketplace. It is important not to lose sight of the fact that anyone can do the obvious. If anyone can do it, however, where is the advantage? Corporate performance management systems are about creating competitive advantage. Their ability to deliver effectiveness gains is the reason many organizations make the decision to invest in them.

To get a sense of where effectiveness plays a role, consider the following questions. What is the value of a penny over or under an analyst's projections? What is the value of knowing about product trends (up or down) as they happen as opposed to once a month? What additional information could be uncovered by accessing enterprise resource planning (ERP), CRM, and supply chain management (SCM) data in context with their financial implications? Current business literature and experience suggests that six "effectiveness" benefits apply to most organizations.

1. *Increased business flexibility.* Having the right information sooner increases options.
2. *Improved planning.* Access to all of the relevant information, together, in the proper context, leads to better planning.
3. *Better decision making.* Think of it as just-in-time information. Just as there is value in manufacturing on a just-in-time basis, there is value in having information when it is needed—not before and not after. Decisions are based on up-to-date data, time is not wasted researching issues that do not exist, and decision makers are not burdened with facts that are not relevant.
4. *Stock market rewards.* The markets reward those companies that demonstrate a firm grasp of their business operations. Shareholders reward companies that demonstrate accuracy in their expectations.
5. *Smarter organizations.* The more widely corporate knowledge is dispersed, the smarter an organization becomes. Unleashing the value and insight of individual functions to an organization en masse increases the organization's intelligence dramatically. An emerging term for this benefit is "return on management" (ROM).
6. *Unified organizations.* When a CPM system is used to link strategy to tactics to measurable results, the organization gains the synergy of everyone working toward a common goal as opposed to imagined personal benefits.

All decision makers should consider these six benefits in the context of their own organization as a minimum requirement in creating an effectiveness list. With this list in hand, the last challenge is to assign some sort of quantifiable value to these seemingly intangible benefits.

Valuing Effectiveness (and Other Intangibles)

The effectiveness gains provided by CPM systems are obviously valuable. The question of how to quantify them, however, is not so obvious. This section describes four techniques for making intangibles real. They include implied value, average expected value, ERP benefit capture, and competitive advantage.

Since these four methods are estimating techniques, certain factions within the organization may mistrust them. The best way to assuage such doubts is to use conservative estimates when drawing correlations or assigning probabilities. The goal is to achieve buy-in to the relevance of the numbers and a general sense of the value to be had when the CPM system is in place.

Implied Value. One technique for estimating value is to find approved projects within an organization that yield comparative value to the proposed project. Use the ROI analysis from the approved project to measure the value of effectiveness gains from CPM systems.

For example, an organization has invested $3 million to create a sales tracking system that speeds up the reporting process from a weekly basis to one that works in real time. The tracking system has saved two weeks; the information that previously took a week to report was already one week old. The implied value is that faster access to information is worth $1.5 million per week gained, or $3 million multiplied by two weeks saved.

Similarly, a proposed CPM system will save a total of three weeks. Closing the books now will take one week instead of three (a savings of two weeks), and reforecasting now will take one week instead of two (a savings of one week). Access to financial information has been improved by three weeks, giving the management application an implied value of $4.5 million. This is a legitimate and conservative value based on already accepted valuation methods established by corporate policy and action independent of this project.

Average Expected Value. This method involves asking the actual people who are going to benefit from the system what they think the benefit is worth. The advantage of this method is that managers are in charge of deciding what the CPM application will do for them specifically. Their involvement will increase the likelihood of acceptance of the project and also may uncover unforeseen benefits. Another advantage to this method is that the estimates are the informed projections of the very people most familiar with the expected benefit. A typical average expected value calculation is shown in Exhibit 7.7.

Enterprise Resource Planning Benefit Capture. Any company that has invested in an ERP system most likely has a fairly detailed business case that was put together for that project. The goal is to go back to this doc-

Exhibit 7.7   "Average expected value" is one technique used to quantify effectiveness gains.

Proposed: CPM Budgeting Application

Function	Potential Value	Probability	Expected Value
Inventory management	$3 million	5 percent	$150,000
Purchasing	$2 million	10 percent	$200,000
Treasury	$2 million	3 percent	$ 60,000
Average Expected Value			$410,000

ument and determine which expected benefits from that project have *not* been realized. One of the most common areas where these lost benefits are found is in the area of information integration, reporting, and analysis. Despite ERP's promise of a single integrated data pool, many organizations have found that they have had to retain certain legacy systems and stand-alone applications for a variety of reasons. The power of CPM systems is that they allow disparate data sources to be brought together and that they improve (if not simply enable for the first time) the data query and reporting capabilities of the ERP implementation. In this instance, the new CPM system can be credited with these already acknowledged and quantified benefits as its own. Similar to implied value calculations, the ERP benefit capture technique is a legitimate and conservative value based on already accepted valuation methods established by corporate policy and action independent of the current project.

Competitive Advantage.   There are fundamentally two ways to increase your competitive advantage: lower costs or increase differentiation. Any analytical application that increases understanding of costs, products, or services is a strategic application, one that increases a company's competitive advantage.

Quantifying investments for competitive advantage is difficult at best when looking at things such as customer web sites or customer relationship management applications. It becomes necessary to try to assign a value to customer loyalty, improved market share, better decision making, and the like. In many instances, even companies with the

159

strongest business cases were able to call on tangible benefits to cover only 40 to 80 percent of the proposed project costs.[6] If those intangible benefits were good enough to justify the remainder of the millions invested in ERP solutions, they certainly belong in an analysis of CPM systems.

To attain an understanding of the appropriate linkages to value and competitive advantage, an organization's mission statement and strategic plan must be evaluated to determine where the themes of unity, shared vision, and improved responsiveness come into play. Given this information, the key executives responsible for implementing this vision should be asked the value of achieving the goal. These conversations can result in the insight required to better link the investment to the organization's strategic vision and develop value estimates for the business case. An additional benefit of this exercise is the early "face time" gained with the key decision makers for the purchase and implementation of the new management system, which gives them the time and opportunity to better understand the value of the investment in ways outside of simple cost savings. Their input will help formulate the effectiveness portion of the business case and provide additional insights that will aid in the ultimate implementation of the systems.

A key strategic benefit of CPM systems is that they unify the organization around a strategic vision. The early work on ROI and the business case through discussions with key executives is the beginning of this benefit.

SUMMARY

Only by having a complete understanding of the business challenges can organizations identify what they hope to accomplish by implementing an enterprise software solution for CPM. This is the cornerstone on which the entire implementation process rests. According to Gartner, those who do successfully implement a corporate performance management solution will be leaders in vision. Gartner also reports that enterprises that want to outperform their industry competitors should immediately start building their CPM strategy.[7]

The pace of change is accelerating in the business environment. The ability to implement corporate strategy and to understand and anticipate changes in the business environment will give an organization true competitive advantage. The tool to achieve this vision is a CPM system that integrates planning, budgeting, forecasting, reporting, and analysis. Today's technology allows maximum value to be extracted from the finance function. Moving from number guardians to full business partner status, finance practitioners should recognize CPM systems as essential tools for their organizations.

Endnotes

1. Nigel Rayner, *Guidelines for Deploying CPM Successfully,* Research Note TG-16-0957, Gartner, Inc., May 3, 2002, 1.
2. Ibid., 4.
3. Nigel Rayner, Frank Buytendijk, and Lee Geishecker, *The Processes That Drive CPM,* Research Note COM-16-2849, Gartner, Inc., May 8, 2001, 2.
4. Rayner, *Guidelines for Deploying CPM Successfully,* 2.
5. Bronwyn Fryer, "The ROI Challenge," *CFO Magazine,* September 1, 1999.
6. Jack M. Keen, "The Courage to Tout Intangibles," EarthWeb.com, June 1, 1999, from web site http://itmanagement.earthweb.com/cio/article/0,,11967_611291,00.html.
7. Nigel Rayner and Lee Geishecker, *Corporate Performance Management: BI Collides with ERP,* Research Note SPA-14-9282, Gartner, Inc., December 17, 2001, 6.

CHAPTER 8

Designing a Corporate Performance Management Solution

DESIGN FRAMEWORK

The next step down the corporate performance management (CPM) road includes visualizing the way in which users will interact with the system and determining the necessary database content. Taking this step involves creating an outline design of the CPM data model, the user interface, and the end-user reports and analyses. The goal is not to select a particular software solution at this stage. Rather, it is to design elements in a way that conforms to the CPM system requirements described in Chapter 5.

Although the CPM system design should concentrate on how the initial phase will be delivered, it must work within the context of the CPM solution that is envisaged a number of phases from now. For example, phase 1 may be the implementation of a budgeting solution, but the design must consider how this solution will be delivered when the reporting and forecasting elements are added in later phases. Correctly designing the system up front will reduce the need for user training when future phases are implemented because the design retains familiar menus and options. Another benefit is that users will sense from day 1 that this system is strategic in scope.

Designing a new system gives organizations an opportunity to do things differently, not do the same old things faster. Corporate performance management systems must focus on strategy implementation, not just process efficiency. Organizations must think beyond the format and capabilities of the system being replaced. "People look for a system to replace an old one they don't like," comments James Sharrett, responsible for the CPM system at Baker and Taylor. "They spend a lot of time trying to get the new one to look, feel, and operate like the old one. CPM is very different. They need to first look at their processes from scratch before implementing a solution. Design the one you want, not the one you had. Otherwise you won't get the benefits."[1]

Today's technologies, the Internet in particular, allow organizations to design systems that are easily navigated by users and provide those users with information from a variety of sources in a variety of ways. No longer do users have to face a series of bland screens and limited options. Take a look at any web site and see the breadth of information that can be delivered. Text, charts, grids of numbers, video, and sound—all can provide the user with different insights on data being displayed. The data do not even have to reside in the same system. For example, it can come from documents, transaction systems, and web sites anywhere in the world, yet all can be delivered within the same page and in a format that requires little or no training to access.

But there is a problem. With so much data, it is easy to bury key information within the detail. Similarly, a multitude of links without any coherent order will confuse users who are trying to follow a process. The design of a CPM system is critical to its usability and, therefore, to the organization's ability to implement and monitor strategy.

In designing the layout of screens and reports, employ someone with a keen eye for design. Those people typically know how to design web sites and are familiar with the technologies involved. Research existing web sites and take note of what works and what does not. Never before has technology given so much flexibility to those building systems. Rarely will technology, if chosen correctly, limit the design. The challenge is to use it effectively.

CPM DATA MODEL

Data Stores and Data Links

All CPM processes operate on the CPM data model, which must embody the organization's strategy. As discussed in Chapter 5, this model contains information about the way the organization operates, such as

Exhibit 8.1   The CPM data model embodies the organization's strategy.

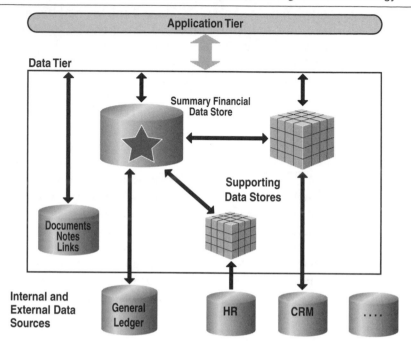

organization structures, activities, products, and projects, and the data from or links to underlying sources (see Exhibit 8.1). The data model holds information in one of three ways: as a summary data store, a detailed supporting store, or a data link.

A CPM system typically consists of one summary data store that contains a mixture of measures, many of which are financial. This store is used to hold plans, budgets, and forecasts at a level of detail determined by the strategic and tactical plans. It also holds actual data to at least the level of detail held by the budget and typically to a more detailed level required for management and financial reporting.

The summary data store typically has multiple detailed supporting stores. Each supporting store focuses on one particular area of the business, at a level of detail required to highlight any material change in the makeup of results. For example, while the summary data store may hold sales by major product groups, a supporting data store would hold sales by individual product and customer. This design would enable users to analyze the way in which various customer groupings buy products over time. Supporting stores automatically feed the summary data store as discussed in Chapter 5.

The third type of information consists of links to documents, web sites, transaction systems, and so on. Links allow users to reference common documents that are connected with information held in any of the data stores as well as to interrogate supporting transaction systems directly. Examples of this type of information include written tactical plans, company reports, and lists of individual transactions for a particular product. Linking allows the CPM system to become a single point of contact for users when analyzing corporate performance.

Content of these data stores should not be limited to internal data. They should include competitor information, market assumptions, and external industry research. The design of this model is critical to the operation of the CPM system. Therefore, it must provide access to these types of information so that users can plan and monitor strategic initiatives.

Summary Data Store Content

The first step in designing the summary data store is to list all the business dimensions and dimension members that will be required. To do this, start by reviewing the strategic and tactical plans. For each tactic and associated goal, determine:

- The base measures and their associated business dimensions that are required to plan and measure the associated goals.
- The assumptions being made about the economic and competitive climate that could impact the achievement of the goals. In some industries this external information can be purchased. Otherwise, some form of research is required. If it cannot be purchased or researched, consider the following adage: If you cannot measure it, do not plan for it.
- The key performance indicators (KPIs) and other leading indicators that will be employed to warn users when a goal is likely to be missed.
- The person or department responsible for delivering the goal. If no one is responsible, then there is nothing to manage.

In the example shown in Exhibit 8.2, an organization has one goal and two tactics related to the strategy of improving sales productivity. The goal of this strategy is to generate revenue of $250,000 for each sales representative by growing the cellular product line by 25 percent over last

Exhibit 8.2 Review the strategic plan at a detailed level.

Strategy: *Improve Sales Productivity*				
Tactic and Goal(s)	**Budget Center**	**Measures**	**Other Related Business Dimensions**	**Frequency of Measurements**
• Achieve sales of $250,000 per sales rep	Sales	Sales Revenue	By person	Monthly
• Grow cellular product line by 25% on last year		Volume	By product	
• Keep sales costs within 15% of total revenues		Cost of Goods Salaries Commission Other Sales Expense		
External business assumption to be monitored: • Average sales per head of peer organization • Cellular market share				
Internal threats • Not enough sales reps • Production can not meet demand		**Leading indicators to monitor** • Number of sales reps and their level of experience • Cellular product line production levels		
Level of detail to support monitoring • Revenue and volume by product, customer, and sales rep		**Level of detail to support forecasting** • Volume by product • Revenue by sales rep		

year and keeping cost of sales to within 15 percent of total revenues. The form has been used to document answers to each of the listed questions.

With this information, measures, dimensions, assumptions, leading indicators, and responsibilities (see Exhibit 8.3) can be determined for planning and tracking the strategic initiative. This process needs to be repeated for each strategy, tactic, and goal. The sample form included in Appendix B can be used to help facilitate this activity. The KPIs that monitor the success of this tactic will come from this list. In this example, the KPIs will be revenue, product growth, cost as a percentage of revenue, number of sales representatives, and product volume as a percentage of production.

The summary data store also will be used to generate management reports and probably financial reports. The reason why this is only prob-

Exhibit 8.3 Review the measures required to
support each strategy, tactic, and goal.

Planning and Tracking by Initiative

Base measures and dimensions:	Revenue to be monitored by person Volume by product COGs, salaries, and commissions by department
External assumptions to be tracked:	Average sales per head in competitor organizations Market share for cellular phones

Leading indicators to be used as alerts:	Number of sales representatives and
	   their level of experience (experienced
	   people tend to sell more)

Responsibility:	Divisional sales managers

able is that, in some organizations, the financial reports are very different from the management reports. This difference typically happens when the company's legal structure bears no resemblance to the management structure. In these cases, it may be worth setting up the financial consolidation as its own separate supporting data store.

Once the measures have been determined for strategy, the organization must identify what additional measures, by the appropriate business dimensions, will be required to generate management and financial reports. From this exercise, the measures and dimensions required to design the summary data store will emerge. Measures include all the base measures, the measures used to track external assumptions, the leading indicators, and those measures used in management and financial reporting.

Next, the measures are organized into schedules. Schedules are simply groupings of accounts that share the same set of dimensions. While doing this, the designer must ensure that strategic initiatives can be planned and tracked individually because this may have an influence on the content of each schedule. Some measures will appear in multiple schedules and need to be linked so that the total value of the measure is held only once. Where measures are financial accounts, the measure type (debit/credit indicator, profit and loss [P&L], balance sheet, currency rate indicator, etc.) should be defined. For calculated measures such as ratios and allocations, the formulae will need to be defined for each schedule where that measure is used.

Finally, the structure of the identified business dimensions needs to be determined. Some dimensions, such as the organization structure, also may have multiple versions, such as geographic, responsibility, and alternative structures. All this definition is necessary to ensure that those people carrying out the evaluation will understand the level of sophistication required.

Supporting Data Store Content

Supporting data stores hold data at a much lower level of detail than the summary data store. They are used to analyze results when strategic goals have been missed or look as if they are likely to be missed. They track the detail behind external assumptions and KPIs as well as the base measures behind each tactic. These data stores almost always include sales and customer information.

In the example given above, the CPM system needs to track how much of each product line is being produced and sold, and to what type of customer. The known threats to success are the number of salespeople, their experience, and the way the market is expected to grow. All these need to be tracked at a detailed level. Product reliability also could affect sales, so some form of quality measure should be monitored and made available as required.

Some of this supporting information could be delivered using a link to the source system rather than by setting up a detailed data store. The choice will depend on what the user wants to do with the information. For something as straightforward as accessing a list of transactions, a link to the underlying data store would be sufficient. But if the user wants to perform analyses such as by product over time, the data should be held in a supporting data store to take advantage of the CPM system's analytical capabilities.

USER INTERFACE

The user interface performs two functions.

1. It leads users through the CPM processes, providing them with relevant information in the right context.

168

2. It draws attention to any issues that arise, such as when a budget submission has been rejected or a goal is in danger of not being met.

No two CPM systems are alike. The look and feel will depend on who the users are and the processes in which they participate. Bearing this in mind, the computer screen shots in this chapter are examples that convey some of the key design points of a CPM system and not a definition of how every CPM system should look.

Layout of the CPM Portal

The first CPM system screen, shown in Exhibit 8.4, is essentially a portal or gateway through which users plan and monitor corporate performance. All CPM systems are web based. That is, a web browser such as Microsoft Internet Explorer is the main mechanism through which users access the system, although options for spreadsheet and personal digital assistant (PDA) device access also may be offered. Because of

Exhibit 8.4 CPM portal.

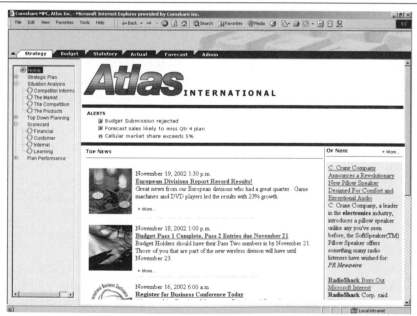

their simplicity, availability, and cost-effectiveness, web browsers have become a particularly productive way of accessing a wide variety of data formats and sources. Good web-based systems free users from being dependent on a particular machine or location, which means users theoretically can access their CPM system from anywhere in the world.

On entering the system, the user will be asked for a user name and password. This combination tailors the screen for that particular user. Most CPM systems have a basic layout that consists of three main areas:

1. Folders or tabs across the top of the screen that represent specific areas of interest to the user
2. A selection of submenus down the left-hand side of the screen
3. A main data viewing area in the center of the screen

In Exhibit 8.4, the folders (or menus) across the top of the screen represent different parts of the CPM process (strategy, budget, etc.). However, they could represent different topics of interest, such as organizational divisions or activities.

Down the left-hand side of the exhibit, submenus or subjects related to the chosen folder or tab appear. When the user selects a menu item, the result or function of that choice appears in the main screen.

The main screen typically displays a result, data entry and review capabilities, the contents of a document, or a function that will initiate a process such as consolidation. Although this layout is common, the content of each part varies widely, as was shown in the systems described in Chapter 6.

In Exhibit 8.4, the home page has been set to show alerts that need the user's attention that have been generated automatically by the system. Below this is general news on company performance and related external news as determined by the administrator. By selecting an alert, the user will be taken to the data that caused the alert to be triggered, where further analyses can be performed. Selecting a "story," such as "C Crane company announcement," will take the user to the associated web page. The user also can choose to go to an appropriate folder (strategy, budget, statutory, etc.) and select any menu item contained within that folder.

Visualizing the Strategic Plan

A good CPM system contains a module that allows the interactive building and visualization of a strategic plan. This module allows strategies and tactics to be discussed and built online during a management plan-

Exhibit 8.5   Building a strategic plan online.

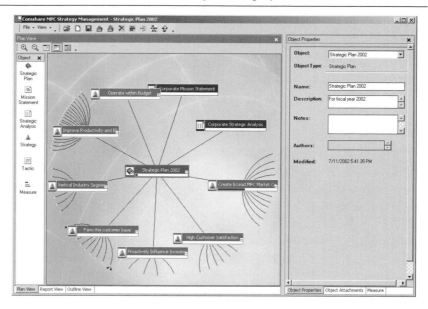

ning meeting. The module shown in Exhibit 8.5 allows management to define its own planning terminology, such as objectives, goals, and tactics. These "objects" can be dragged onto the screen and attached as required to build the strategic plan.

As each object is selected, the user answers a series of questions that help management define the plan in detail. For example, when defining a tactic, the module prompts for information on goals, the time span in which those goals are to be achieved, and the person responsible (see Exhibit 8.6).

Some strategic planning modules allow different parts of the plan to be built remotely and then attached at the appropriate place when completed. This ability provides support for organizations where the development of tactical plans is devolved but that need to tie into the overall strategic plan. Goals entered here can be used to set top-down targets as part of a budgeting process. While this view of the strategic plan is excellent for senior management, it can cause confusion among budget holders. The reason is that the layout is not based on organizational responsibility and the budget holders may not understand how their responsibilities impact the plan.

Exhibit 8.6   Leading the user through the strategic planning process.

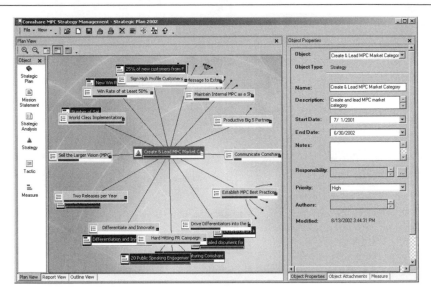

Exhibit 8.7   Clarifying the relationship between departmental activities and organizational strategy.

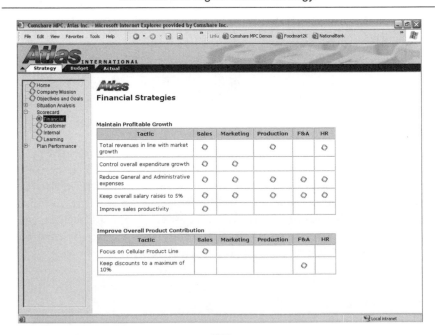

Showing Departmental Impact on Strategy

Exhibit 8.7, however, displays a good example of how a system can clarify the impact of departmental activities on organizational strategy. In this example, the tactics that support each strategy are displayed in a grid, while the placement of an icon within the grid shows which departments have responsibility for delivering the goal.

When the user selects an icon by clicking on it, the department's specific measures for the tactic are displayed, as are the actual and planned results and a color-coded variance (see Exhibit 8.8). This same concept can be used to budget by activity or by strategic initiative. On budget data entry, selecting a tactic displays just those measures and the appropriate business dimensions to which the user must submit a budget.

Leading Users through the Process

Once a process has been initiated, web-based systems make it easy to tell users what they need to do and when. Users can access instructions, timetables, and tailored help messages that can dramatically lower support needs (see Exhibit 8.9).

Exhibit 8.8   CPM systems present useful information
in useful contexts for each system user.

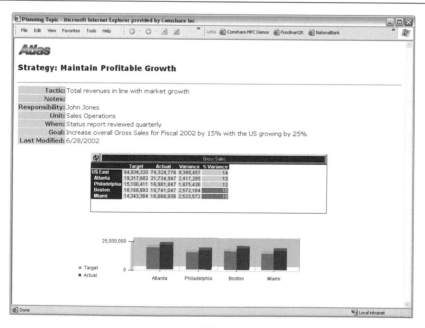

Exhibit 8.9 CPM systems guide users through processes.

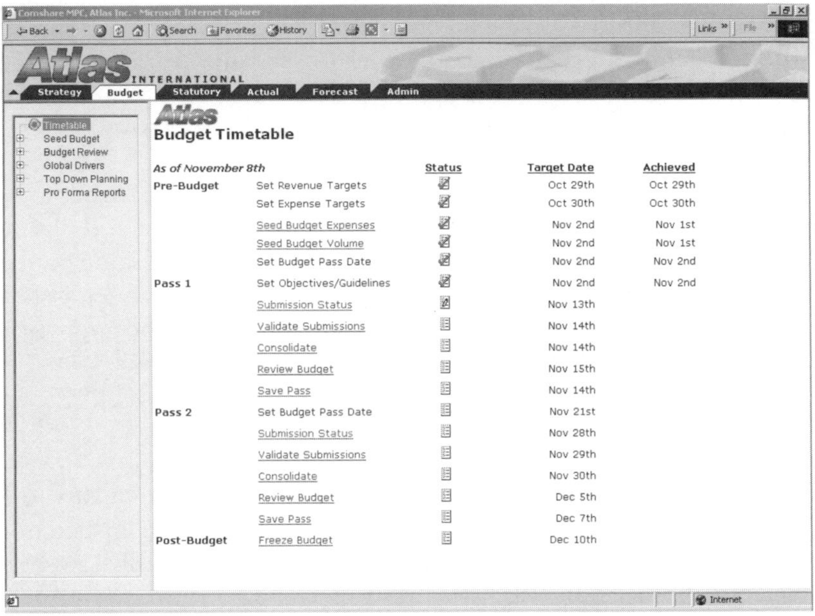

In addition to enabling users to plan and monitor by tactic, CPM systems provide functionality that helps improve the way in which users communicate and perform processes. For example, a solution might enable the automatic checking of budget submissions against management's guidelines and notify users if their submissions are outside those guidelines. These systems also support the collection of text so users can explain why certain goals have not been met. Similarly, management can give reasons why submissions have been rejected, allowing a collaborative dialogue to be set up between users (see Exhibit 8.10).

REPORTS AND ANALYSES

Reviewing Methodology

Corporate performance management systems contain more data than can be analyzed; the last thing busy organizations need is a slice-and-dice tool that their employees can use to wander aimlessly—and endlessly—

Exhibit 8.10 CPM enables collaborative
dialogues throughout the organization.

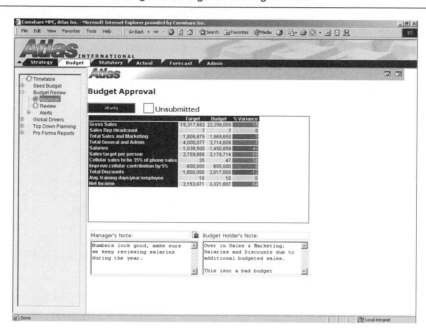

through countless results. They need focus to be efficient and effective. Therefore, it is important to notify users about items that are outside of guidelines or expected results and what areas need further attention.

Similarly, reports can easily mask problems by not showing abnormal trends that are buried in the detail. In Chapter 3, a methodology was discussed that could be used to review the validity of a budget. Rather than looking straight at the bottom line, for example, a logical review of key questions could immediately highlight whether the budget is even attainable. Once this has been done, time then can be spent looking at the bottom line and determining how to improve it.

The same concept applies whether reviewing a budget, a forecast, or actual results. Determine what needs to be assessed and reviewed, and then lead users through this review process (see Exhibit 8.11). Bear in mind that "traditional" reports that are made up of just numbers do not necessarily convey information that is easy to digest. The CPM systems allow the imaginative use of visualization techniques that enables users to assess large volumes of data, helping them to determine which areas need closer study.

Exhibit 8.11 Using technology to lead users through a review process.

Exhibit 8.12 Corporate objectives and tactics by department.

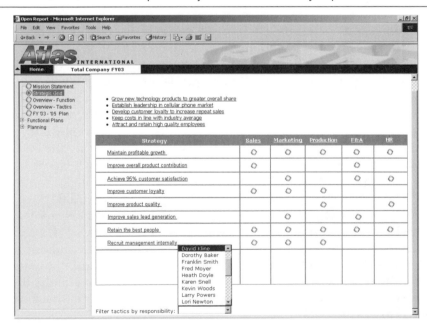

Reviewing Strategic Success

Strategic success should be a focus of CPM systems. The systems can do this in some innovative ways. In the next example, the corporate objectives and tactics that apply to each department are shown as a grid. Selecting any of these would show the appropriate measures and results. This screen also allows users to investigate results by person, security permitting, irrespective of department or tactic (see Exhibit 8.12).

When a user's name is selected (see Exhibit 8.13), a list of the individual's specific tactics—color-coded to show the current status of actual versus plan—appears. Selecting any of these items then reveals the detailed results, which can be investigated further.

Another way of reviewing the total strategic plan is shown in Exhibit 8.14. This overview chart shows the four areas of a Balanced Scorecard. These four areas are then broken down into the various strategies and tactics. In the screen shot, only the financial aspect of the scorecard has been expanded to reveal each color-coded tactic and the status of each department's success in attaining its goal. Selecting the department by clicking on its name reveals the detailed measures and how they compare to the plan, which is presented in a more traditional-looking report. This is a

Exhibit 8.13 Measures and results by person.

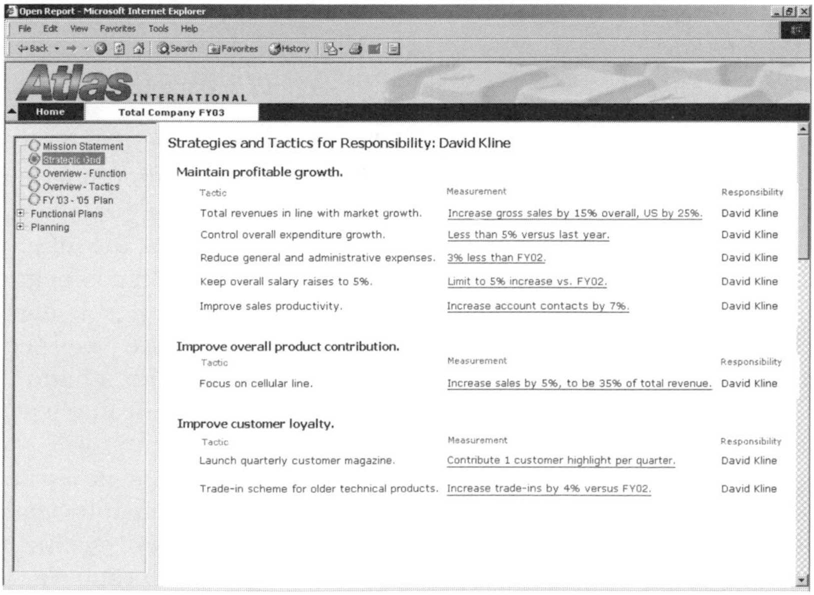

Exhibit 8.14 An overview allows the system user to quickly see the entire enterprise.

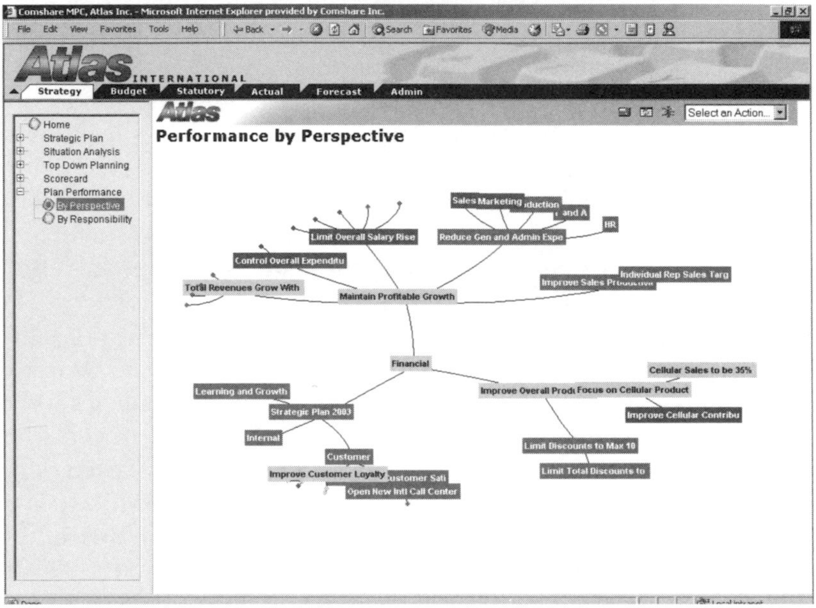

prime example of how technology can show quickly which parts of the plan are not working so that attention can be focused on them.

Reviewing Status against Competitors

Most organizations' strategies include beating the competition, so it follows that results must be reviewed in light of the competition's performance. To do this requires contrasting results and providing intelligence in a form that is easy to access. In Exhibit 8.15, for example, the summary data store holds updated key performance information on competitors, which is compared to the organization's current performance. Using the provided buttons allows the user to change the measure being compared. This is currently set to "Return on Assets." Similarly, a button allows the selection of a competitor and displays the latest intelligence about that competitor on the CPM system screen.

Another way to show how well the organization is performing against competitors is to show the trend in winning. This information would come from a supporting data store fed by a sales tracking system. Exhibit 8.16 is an example that shows the win rate ratio by sales

Exhibit 8.15 Comparing results with competitors' performances.

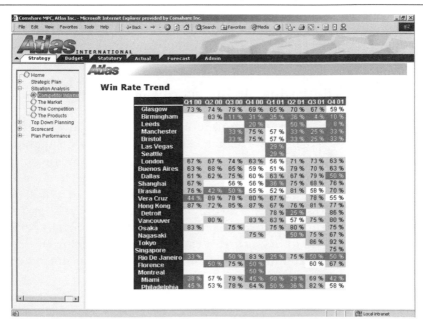

Exhibit 8.16 Win rate ratio by sales department.

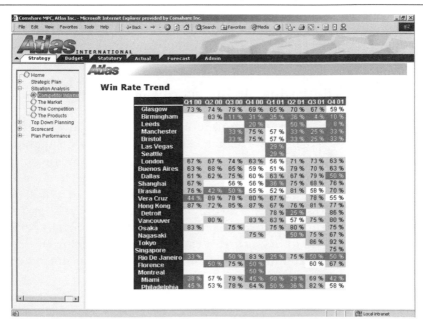

Exhibit 8.17   CPM clarifies the impact of
currency rate fluctuations on results.

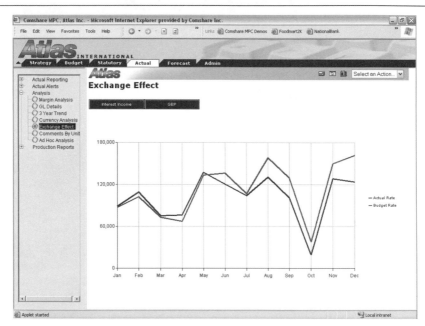

department. This ratio is a leading indicator and can help focus management's attention on actions that will improve future performance.

Reviewing the Impact of Currency

Currency fluctuations in an organization that trades in many countries can easily mask actual performance. All CPM systems are capable of working in multiple base currencies and with multiple versions of exchange rates. In Exhibit 8.17, this capability has been put to good use in comparing actual performance at both the budget and actual rate and plotting the result. Here a favorable movement in exchange rates has improved actual performance at a consolidated level. Performance had nothing to do with strategy. Other reports can be developed that show, by country, which units benefited from unexpected exchange rate differences.

Exhibit 8.18   Color-coding makes it easy to spot problems.

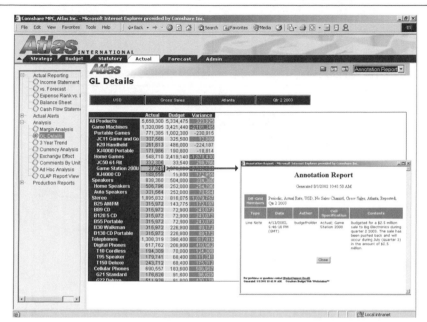

Drilling through to Underlying Systems

At some point, users will want access to the underlying transaction systems to uncover the detail behind any result. In Exhibit 8.18, the CPM system has ranked sales by product and has color-coded the variances from the plan. One of the products has underperformed and is easily identifiable with color-coding. A supporting note entered by the sales department provides an explanation for why this result occurred.

The system also provides a way to find out directly from the sales ledger what actual transactions took place during this period. Simply selecting the appropriate icon at the top of the screen commands the CPM system to interrogate the sales ledger and provide an answer (see Exhibit 8.19).

Exhibit 8.19 Drill down into transactional systems
to see underlying issues or problems.

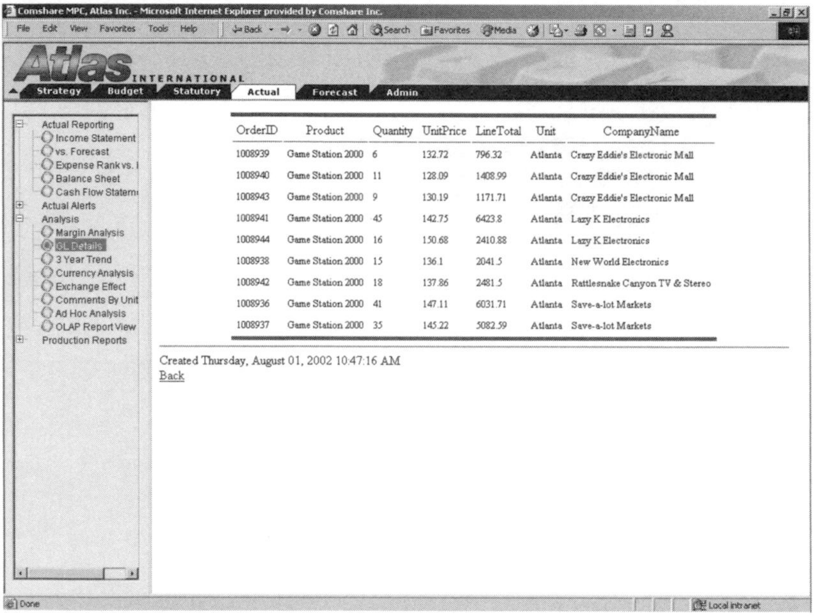

SUMMARY

When designing a CPM system, organizations must fight the urge to re-create their old, problem-ridden systems. They must ensure that the phase 1 design can incorporate the next several phases of the CPM project without major modification. Doing this may mean preplanning all of the folders and menus required in a much later version of the system so that subsequent versions add to the original design.

The use of charts and color-coding can greatly improve the understanding of results. Hire a professional to create the color palette, design icons, select fonts, and design a general layout that is logical and user-friendly. Where possible, conform to existing standards, such as those found in Microsoft products. Stick with the scheme consistently throughout the application to reduce training time as each additional phase is rolled out.

Think carefully about the way in which users will review results and navigate through the various processes. Supply plenty of help screens within easy reach of users, but do not let the screens hinder the more experienced users. If the organization already has a corporate information portal, then make the CPM system part of it. If a portal does not already exist, make the CPM system the portal through which all other information is accessed.

Make the system informative by putting links into related documents and web sites. The goal is to ensure that users access the system on a regular if not continuous basis. Make sure that it is the only way to access any aspect of corporate performance. If other systems are used to create performance reports, then ensure that those reports can be accessed only through the CPM system. In this way, users will become experienced and the organization can deliver more information with less fear of it getting missed.

Invite users to continually contribute to the design of the system. Place a comments page within the system that allows users to e-mail suggestions to the CPM administrator regarding additional information they would like to see, but always make sure the focus of the system remains on the implementation of strategy. Monitor which portal pages get accessed and which do not. At some stage, it will be beneficial to lose pages that are just cluttering up the system. The same is true of the supporting data stores.

Finally, do not be afraid of starting again when it comes to the data model. Many of the early CPM adopters found that their first systems contained too much information that was not focused. Even if an organization manages to get the system 90 percent right in the first release, the changing economic environment and customer needs will see to it that the measures will not be right in the medium term. Corporate performance management systems are fairly quick to build, once organizations know what they want. Obviously, there is a cost to changing the model in terms of effort but there is an even bigger cost if an organization is hampered in implementing strategy through a system that does not meet its needs.

Endnote

1. Interview with James Sharrett, financial planning and systems manager for Baker and Taylor during its CPM system selection and implementation, July 25, 2002. See Chapter 6 for more information.

CHAPTER 9

Implementing a Corporate Performance Management Solution

KNOWLEDGE AND CHOICES

Once an organization has a corporate performance management (CPM) road map and has decided on the contents of the first phase of implementation, an implementation plan can be created. To do this successfully, the business must operate within the confines of a software package, understand and communicate what actions are necessary for implementation, ensure that those actions are carried out, and educate users affected by the new processes about their roles and responsibilities.

Implementation of any enterprise-wide software application can be costly in terms of money and resources. In addition, solutions that do not meet the business's requirements can inflict great damage by adversely impacting efficiency and effectiveness. This chapter is provided to help organizations understand the solution choices, prepare project plans, evaluate software, and understand the way in which projects can be controlled to minimize failure.

PROJECT PLANNING

Avoiding Project Failure

Before considering any software solution, carefully plan the project. Many times issues unrelated to software are the cause of implementation failures. In most cases these failures could have been avoided had the project been managed correctly. During a series of courses held by the American Management Association on using technology to implement planning, budgeting, and reporting solutions, participants cited seven conditions as the major causes of project failure.

1. *Insufficient cooperation.* Differing priorities and internal politics can play a part in starving the project of the right resources or in removal of support when it is most needed. Withholding information is a related form of opposition, which can result in organizational members not getting involved or not fully understanding their roles. All CPM systems are enterprise-wide and require the full cooperation and support of management to be successful.
2. *Solving the wrong problems.* For example, to shorten the reporting cycle, an organization may implement an automated reporting and distribution system. If the data are never available on time, however, the organization has not solved the right problem. All CPM systems must be targeted at solving the real problems. When building a CPM road map, it is essential to clearly identify the real problems.
3. *Not having the right skills.* Implementing CPM systems requires cross-functional expertise on processes, information technology, and business needs. If any one of these is missing, that lack of skill will jeopardize the success of the project.
4. *Lack of the right tools.* In terms of CPM, this lack means not having the right software and technology infrastructure. Building a budgeting solution using just spreadsheets or older discrete solutions may work well enough for a few users submitting budgets but will fail when stretching it to implement a CPM solution across an enterprise.
5. *Not anticipating and managing changes or add-on issues.* Management systems are complex due to the depth and breadth of detail involved. Therefore, changes will arise. Implementations

185

from both a technology and a project management view must accommodate change accordingly. When change occurs, it is vital to consider, understand, and manage the add-on effect of that change. When not actively managed, change can result in a loss of focus and a solution that does not solve the original problem.

6. *Working with wrong assumptions.* In large projects, particularly those that span organizational functions, those involved or affected may not know fully the objective or scope of the project. This lack of knowledge or assumed knowledge can cause major problems because individual expectations may not be met. Decisions could be made without knowing the impact it will have on others and on the overall implementation. Failure to clarify assumptions can result in organizational confusion and distrust in those managing the project, both of which will impact the project's likelihood of success.

7. *Tackling too large a project.* By their nature, CPM systems impact most parts of the organization. Trying to implement CPM using the "big bang" approach will result in failure; implementation will take too long and is unlikely to meet management's expectations. The longer a project takes, the more likely the organization is to lose interest. Delivering too much new functionality to users at one time also can be frustrating for them. Implementing CPM is best tackled in small phases. Each phase delivers quick, visible benefits to the organization and encourages further developments. It also allows users to become comfortable with the new system a little at a time. Even if an anticipated business benefit fails to develop, the phased approach means that little time and resources will have been wasted. Treating CPM implementation as a series of smaller projects enables critical issues to be addressed sooner and allows the organization to adjust priorities and deliver real business benefits throughout the entire process.

Creating a CPM Development Team

The team that drives the CPM development initiative is key to its successful implementation. Chapter 7 described the team responsible for formulating the CPM road map. This team may need to be extended, or a new team created, when it is time to develop the solution. The CPM development team needs to have members that can carry out the roles shown in Exhibit 9.1.

Exhibit 9.1 CPM development team roles and responsibilities.

Roles	Responsibilities
Project Sponsor	Ensures that the project manager receives the necessary resources
	Verifies that the project stays on course
	Reports progress to senior management
Project Manager	Organizes all implementation resources
	Reports on actual and forecasted progress to the CPM implementation team
	Reports issues that threaten the project's success
	Ensures that project deliverables are completed on time and at an acceptable level of quality
	Acts as a liaison between departments affected by the new system
	Organizes the transfer of the completed system from the development environment to the production environment
	Organizes training
Business Representative	Ensures that the CPM system meets business requirements
	Makes certain that the system remains within the scope of the business case that was used to obtain project funding
User Representative	Verifies that the resulting system will meet end-user needs
	Participates in acceptance testing
	Critiques and contributes to the content and quality of user training and associated manuals
	Ensures the availability of adequate business staff and procedures to support the resulting system in a live environment
IT Representative	Makes certain that the system meets current and future IT standards
	Provides development and production environments
	Delivers procedures to move the system between environments
	Ensures that there is adequate IT staff and procedures to support the resulting system in a live environment
	Enables all interactions between the new system and existing systems
	Provides resources to fine-tune database performance

With the exception of the project manager, these roles must be carried out by staff within the organization and should not be given to a third party. The CPM development team is responsible for the specification, selection, and implementation of the CPM solution and must have the appropriate skills and authority with which to perform these duties.

Once software selection has taken place, the team will need to be augmented with implementation staff whose responsibilities include transforming specifications into a practical, working solution; helping create end-user and administrator documentation; and conducting end-user training. It is useful to recruit some of the implementation staff from the team that will be responsible for support once the application goes live. Doing this will assist in the setting up of an effective help desk as well as ensure that the resulting system can be maintained and extended without reliance on a third party.

Project Scope

Once the development team is in place, they must understand and agree on what needs to be accomplished in both the short- and long-term life of the solution. The completed CPM road map should already summarize requirements. Now they need to be communicated to the development team and potential software vendors. Creating a project scope document will help facilitate the software selection and subsequent solution development.

The project scope deals with the constraints under which the solution must operate and the objectives that must be achieved for success. Within the project scope, avoid defining the exact solution too narrowly. Leave room to consider the input of software vendors. Take advantage of their experience with providing similar solutions at other companies. Appendix C contains a sample project scope document that can be used by the project team.

BUILD OR BUY?

Organizations have two choices with regard to CPM software: build their own or buy a packaged solution. The pros and cons to each option must be fully understood for the enterprise to make the correct choice for its particular needs and circumstances.

Building a CPM Software Solution

Building a solution involves choosing a technology platform and creating all the necessary components for CPM. Someone must create the business model, write programs and procedures to calculate business rules, develop a user interface through which the various CPM processes will be controlled, and define how reports and analyses will be created. Organizations taking this approach may combine a number of industry standard technologies, such as a spreadsheet for reporting and an OLAP (Online Analytical Processing) database for building the model, to create their solution.

Pros.   Benefits of building a CPM solution include:

- The organization gets exactly what it specifies. There is no requirement to compromise on the functionality or appearance because the system can be tailored to its exact needs.
- The development of the solution is under the organization's direct control. It determines the order and level of functionality to be delivered.

Cons.   Reasons why organizations should carefully consider whether they want to build their own CPM system include:

- The resulting solution will be limited by their experience and technological expertise. Technologies come and go at a frightening pace, and many information technology (IT) departments just cannot keep up with developments. Similarly, organizations rely only on the perspective of their own systems and practices, which may not necessarily reflect industry best practices.
- Because all components and associated functionality will need to be built and integrated as a whole, implementing a "homegrown" system will almost certainly take much longer than a purchased system.
- Homegrown solutions are expensive. While the initial purchase price of the technology may seem low, organizations must factor in the cost of manpower to build, test, and deliver the solution to accurately describe the cost of the system.
- Custom-built CPM solutions can be expensive to maintain over time as the technology platforms change. For example, if XML (Extensible Markup Language) becomes the accepted standard

189

for integrating systems, the CPM system also will need to change if it is to support a future enterprise resource planning (ERP) implementation that adopts this standard. This may mean a major redevelopment.

- The organization will be required to perform its own beta testing, quite often in the "live" environment.

Buying a Software Solution

Buying a solution involves the selection of a software package designed for CPM, which is then configured for use within the organization. Typically CPM packages come with a flexible business model and an administrator interface that greatly simplifies the setting up of the business rules, user interface, reports, and analyses. Because these packages are designed for CPM, much of the functionality is supplied out of the box. Building the system generally is just a matter of selecting options.

Pros. Provided that the right vendor is chosen—that is, one that has a track record of delivering successful CPM solutions—the benefits of this approach include:

- Organizations benefit from the experience of other companies both now and in the future. The larger software vendors work with hundreds of companies. They use that experience in ongoing development and refinement of their solutions.
- The solution can be implemented faster because things such as the user interface and much of the functionality is already built. Enabling the functionality should be a matter of choosing from a list of options.
- The software may provide solutions to issues the organization did not think of solving with the new system. For example, the solution may come with an analysis tool that allows end users to analyze customer relationship management (CRM) data, even though this functionality was not sought initially.
- The system has been beta tested by someone else, has been proven to work, and therefore can be delivered on time. Someone else has used it, and the success of the implementation and usage of the system can be measured before embarking on a costly implementation process.

- These packages generally are designed to accommodate change. They allow finance staff to make changes, which are then incorporated throughout the system quickly and easily. The best packages also perform integrity checks that ensure a change does not give ambiguous or otherwise problematic results. For example, an intelligent solution will not allow the same unit—such as "European Operations"—to appear twice within an organizational structure, avoiding the erroneous doubling of all results and figures related to this unit.

- Over time, purchased solutions are much less expensive to maintain. Software vendors are able to spread the cost of application maintenance across hundreds of customers. Therefore, for a relatively small fee, customers have a dedicated team of professionals continually working to enhance their solution.

- These systems tend to be "future proofed" to some extent. It is in the vendors' interest to keep their solutions working on the latest technology platforms so that customers will continue to pay annual maintenance fees. Should a major technology shift occur, successful vendors would develop newer products and provide migration options to existing customers.

Cons. Although there are reasons to consider building a CPM system rather than buying one, careful vendor and system selection can negate these issues:

- Organizations may have to compromise on features and user interfaces. Generally users must work in the way the system was designed to be used. Otherwise, they will not get the benefits.

- The underlying technology used by the vendor, such as the database, may be proprietary or not one that is used within the organization. This fact could lengthen the time needed for integration with existing systems and necessitate learning and gaining expertise in a different technology.

- Up-front costs are very visible and may make it harder to get the necessary approvals to proceed with a project.

- If the vendor misunderstands the organization's needs, the system may not perform as expected or, in some cases, may not work at all.

- The product may be unreliable and support services unusable, resulting in a solution that is not viable.

191

- The vendor may discontinue the product being used or may even go out of business. Then the solution will no longer be supported, and the costs of reimplementation using a different product will be incurred.

Given the complexity and breadth of CPM solutions, most CPM packages offer an open approach. That is, the software has built-in functionality on top of a mainstream database that allows organizations to build extra capabilities if required. In these cases, the chosen vendor must confirm whether it will support the development of extra functionality within its application. If it cannot provide this confirmation, the resulting solution could well be the worst of both worlds; the cons from both the build and buy options will be present, while none of the pros will be guaranteed. Another danger facing organizations is that they may find themselves selecting a package that, based on marketing materials, appears to support CPM but was not designed for this purpose. This approach also will attract all the cons of both the build and buy options but very few of the pros—and all at a premium price.

The "build" or "buy" choice will depend on each organization's circumstances and must be considered carefully. The balance of this chapter provides guidance for organizations that decide to purchase a CPM package.

SELECTING A CPM PACKAGE

Once the project scope has been fully developed, the organization—especially someone from the implementation team—must critically evaluate vendors. This is no time to make a decision on gut instinct. After all, most vendors are highly adept at presenting their solutions in the best possible light. To choose the solution that will truly meet the organization's business needs, the team must base its selection on knowing the facts about the product being offered and how it will be implemented within the organization. The evaluation process should include vendor research, product research, detailed evaluation, assessing implementation effort, negotiation, and vendor selection.

Vendor Research

A number of organizations provide advice and information about CPM solution vendors, ranging from specialized finance magazines to industry analysts who review and publish findings on vendor solutions. Be aware that vendors themselves influence most free sources of information. Management consultancies will carry out evaluations on behalf of an organization for a suitable fee, but the organization needs to investigate whether the consultancy has strategic alliances with particular vendors. Always be aware that recommendations may not be as impartial as one might expect.

According to Gartner, software vendors promoting CPM solutions fall into four categories:

1. *Traditional business intelligence vendors.* These vendors are strong on enabling people to access data but have limited experience when it comes to supporting business processes.
2. *Niche or specialty vendors.* These vendors concentrate on one particular process, such as budgeting or consolidation. Because of their narrow focus, they typically cannot support true CPM.
3. *Integration or ERP vendors.* These vendors are making huge investments in CPM but tend to be limited by the complexity and closed architecture of their existing solutions.
4. *Hybrid vendors.* These vendors combine their process expertise with a general business intelligence (BI) platform. This group is also making large investments in CPM, but developments tend to be restricted by the vendor's size.

Potential vendors must be committed to CPM and provide a proven, modern solution. To establish this, ask these questions:

- What is their background? Do they have expertise and a proven, positive history in the area of CPM, or are they just jumping on the bandwagon?
- Did they develop the solution they are selling, or are they partnering with someone else? Partnerships can break down, so examine and assess support arrangements and commitments. How do they resolve support issues when it is not clear in which product the problem occurs?
- How long has the solution been around? Is it an old solution that is about to be replaced? Will the product still be around five years from now? Many vendors are in the process of replacing their old, discrete solutions with those designed for CPM, so find out which product is being offered.
- Do they use current technologies? In other words, find out whether they use web protocols and mainstream database technologies. What is the vendor's vision for future platform support?

In the past, have they successfully migrated customers from one technology to another?
- What do industry analysts say about a vendor and its product? Who are the vendor's customers, and what do they say about the solution?
- Can the vendors support us? Do they operate where the users are located? Can they support us internationally in local languages and at any time of day or week? Do they have an appropriate number of experienced staff? There is no value in having the best solution when it cannot be supported or has a limited life.

Product Research and Detailed Evaluation

Most vendors provide overviews of their applications via a web site, brochure, seminar, or personal demonstration. The organization's objective here is to see, at a summary level, which vendors are best able to meet its requirements and should be the subjects of a more detailed evaluation.

Once the list has been narrowed down and vendors have been invited to speak about their products, organizations should beware of vendors that arrive armed with canned demonstrations. Naturally, such a demonstration will show the vendor's strengths but may not reveal how the solution will—or will not—address the organization's business problems. Instead of agreeing to view a canned presentation, inform the vendor about the basic business needs as described in the project scope document. Ask for a demonstration on how a given solution will meet those specific needs. A good vendor will respect an organization's time and get straight to the point.

During the detailed software evaluation, the organization will want to confirm or discover whether:

- The product has the functionality and capability to solve both the current and future requirements.
- The staff supporting the project can maintain it.
- The solution's capabilities have been oversold.
- The product delivers additional capabilities and features that will give the business additional advantages.
- The vendor is viable. Verify its understanding of the business issues to be resolved, its expertise in the area of CPM, the likelihood

of establishing a relationship that will work for both organizations, and its commitment to CPM.

- The future direction and life of the product will support your organization's vision for CPM.
- Other organizations are using the product for CPM and what business benefits they have obtained.

Evaluate the data model capability using a realistic full-size application. Ensure the model being demonstrated has an organizational structure, product or customer dimensions, and measures that are similar in number to those being proposed. Building a new system containing a few measures may look fine in the demonstration, but it may not translate into a real-world application involving many measures and multiple users. After all, a spreadsheet would perform very well with a small model, yet most organizations know what happens when these are turned into real-world, multiple-user systems. Ask to see how measures are created and dimensioned by different levels of detail. For example, ask to see how revenues can be tracked by customer and product, while the balance sheet is tracked just by operational unit.

Ensure the system shown is set up so the maximum number of people involved in the process can use it. A multiuser system often looks substantially different from a single-user system. Make sure the system is able to cope with the number of users expected in the next 12 to 18 months as the system evolves. Check the effort required to roll out the system to a new user; web-based systems should make this easy.

Next verify that the product can accommodate all the processes that will be required by the final CPM solution. Chapter 3 described the most basic processes that should be supported. Appendix D contains a functional checklist that can be used to perform this task. If the system lacks any of these capabilities, consider whether the solution is really capable of supporting true corporate performance management and meeting the organization's CPM needs.

Next review the solution's ability to generate reports, highlight exceptions, and empower users to create their own reports and analyses. Some vendors do not provide these capabilities themselves but rely on third-party products. This design can cause problems for the organization because data must be duplicated, separate models must be maintained, and an additional technology must be learned. In addition to the extra effort this solution involves, data integrity is compromised because there is no longer a single version of the truth. Also, many third-party viewing tools have no financial understanding, which means variances and summations over time will be wrong because the system does not understand the difference between debits and credits, profits and losses, and balance sheet accounts.

Learn whether users must look through detail reports to spot exceptions or whether the system provides automated alerts as the exceptions occur. Alerting capabilities eliminate the possibility of exceptions remaining undetected and save the user time normally spent looking for exceptions that may or may not exist. Also determine whether the production and delivery of reports can be automated. This option can save substantial amounts of time and effort.

Continue by exploring the solution's end-user analysis capabilities. Can users drill down into a variance and then calculate new analyses? A good way to discover this is to ask the vendor, during a demonstration, to create a variance without any advance warning. For example, ask the vendor to calculate actual/budget variance percentages for all companies. Sort the result to show the top 10 performers by revenue. Then show this for total costs. Find out whether this variance can be color-coded and/or presented as a chart.

Account for the fact that different users need different ways of analyzing data. Some users prefer spreadsheets, while others would like to have data available on their personal digital assistant. How does the application support these users, and how much effort will be required by an administrator?

Next review the solution's architecture. What technologies does the system use to hold the data model and provide end-user access? Are these mainstream technologies, or will new skills be needed to maintain and support the system? Determine whether the architecture and technologies involved fit in with IT policy. Problems can be avoided if the data model uses the same technology as existing transactional/ERP and CRM applications. This solution greatly simplifies data integration and ongoing support. Also explore whether the system design is sound and will be able to expand with the organization without trouble.

Investigate whether data are duplicated at any stage. Duplicating data means that transfers need to be set up, maintained, and run, with the chance that someone may not be seeing the latest version of the data. A good way to check what happens in the vendor's system is to enter a number as a budget holder and then ask to see that exact same number in an actual budget variance report from a controller's point of view.

Finally, determine whether the software easily supports change. A good way to test this is to ask the vendor, without prior notice, to make a change. For example, ask the vendor to add a new organizational unit, reorganize the product structure, and then check to see what effort is involved in getting those changes reflected in the user interface and associated reports. All CPM systems should be able to cope with these changes and automatically reflect them in data entry screens, reports, and analyses.

Other Considerations

In addition to carefully scrutinizing the operational aspects of the product, the organization should carefully consider the true cost of ownership of a solution. Investigate the vendor's relationships with existing clients, understand the future product direction, assess implementation effort, and understand exactly what the vendor proposes to deliver.

When understanding the true cost of ownership, the initial software purchase is unlikely to be the largest cost incurred. Take into account implementation, user training, and software maintenance costs. Product life also could be a major issue. If the vendor discontinues the product and supplies the latest product at "no charge," it is likely that the existing system will have to be thrown away and reimplemented with the new product. This is very expensive in terms of time, effort, and resources.

Next talk to references. Most vendors have impressive client lists. However, organizations should research how many of those clients implemented CPM, not just a planning package or budgeting software. If the vendor has not implemented successful CPM solutions before, its experience will be gained at the CPM team's expense. The project team should verify that the vendor's reference customers have implemented applications of the same size and complexity as the one the organization wants to implement. Find out the references' real cost of implementation and the kind of support they received from the vendor.

Next investigate the vendor's vision for its CPM product. All CPM applications are relatively new. While the vendor's marketing literature may reflect CPM, does the product being offered truly reflect it today? If not, will the vendor be selling an updated product six or 12 months from now? If so, what will happen to the applications of existing customers? Will the newer product be supplied free of charge? Will the newer product have the same level of functionality? Will it convert the existing data model, user interface, and all reports with no effort? Will users and support staff need to be retrained? Without definitive answers to these questions, organizations risk implementing an old product that may lead to failure and additional cost. In a related vein, organizations should never rely on a feature or function that will be available in the "next" version. Software vendors regularly miss deadlines and release products that are not as functional as they were described in the prerelease plan.

As the evaluation continues, the CPM team should assess the implementation effort involved in a vendor's solution. Discover whether the vendor has a methodology that will guarantee a successful implementation. It is easier to perform a simple demonstration than it is to implement a robust, enterprise-wide CPM solution in an organization's specific IT environment. There is no point in choosing the world's best technology if it cannot be delivered as a working, viable solution.

Find out what resources will be required to deliver a working solution and how much effort will be involved. Also find out whether the vendor is prepared to guarantee the cost of implementation. Take time to plan the implementation with each vendor, and make sure you understand the efforts that will be required on both sides. See Appendix E for a sample list of activities that will need to take place.

Finally, the CPM team must understand exactly what each vendor is proposing. Is it simply selling software? How much consultancy time will it provide? If consultancy is involved, what is being guaranteed—the delivery of a solution, or simply an estimate of time required? What levels of support are included in the price, and what other services are provided at extra cost?

It will be easiest to compare vendors if they are required to submit proposals in a standardized format. Appendix F presents an example of a standardized format. Only when the organization has completed all the processes and assessed all the implications thoroughly will the CPM team be able to make an informed decision. Appendix G provides a scorecard that can be used to compare software vendors side by side.

CONTROLLING THE IMPLEMENTATION

Implementation Methodology

When a third-party software vendor is involved, the implementation success results from the partnership that is formed between the organization and the vendor. In some cases a management consultancy also may be involved, but all parties must work together for an implementation to be successful.

Exhibit 9.2 A CPM implementation methodology describes how vendors and clients will work together.

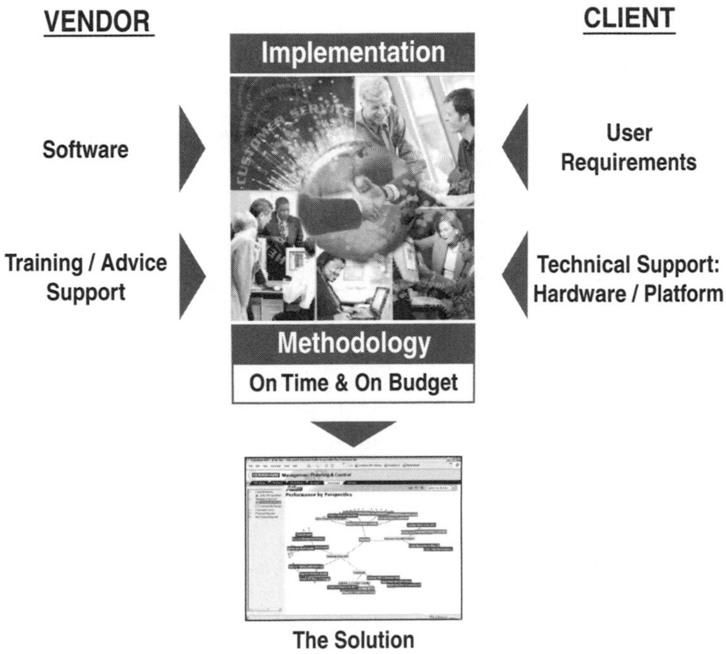

VENDOR

CLIENT

Implementation

Software

User
Requirements

Training / Advice
Support

Technical Support:
Hardware / Platform

Methodology

On Time & On Budget

The Solution

Each party brings special skills to the venture. The software vendor supplies software, training, and technical advice, while the organization supplies the requirements and the hardware/software infrastructure on which the solution will run. An implementation methodology describes the process by which they will work together to deliver the solution on time and within budget (see Exhibit 9.2).

Methodologies define the roles and responsibilities of the development team members and outline the necessary steps in the process. Each step has a starting point and a set of inputs that usually are derived from the output of previous steps. Each step ends with the completion of its deliverables. Exhibit 9.3 illustrates some steps and deliverables for a CPM project.

Each of these steps can be broken down into a series of activities. Appendix E provides a sample task list. A typical CPM project has at least 32 activities of which only six are related to software development. Although today's software packages can save time in implementation, they cannot replace the remaining activities. Eliminating any of these

Exhibit 9.3 Process steps and deliverables for a CPM project.

Step	Deliverable
Project Scope: Defines the problems being experienced and the scope of a new system.	*Project Scope Document*
Application Specification: Defines in detail exactly how the system will be put together, including how data will be gathered, processed, and reported back to users, and how the system will look and feel.	*Detailed Specification*
Technical Design: Defines how the system will be implemented in harmony with the organization's current IT infrastructure.	*Technical Design Document*
Development: Builds the system using the software package and writes any additional code that may be required.	*Draft Solution*
Acceptance Testing: Tests the system thoroughly according to a predetermined plan to check that it performs as specified.	*Signed Acceptance Test Plan*
System Rollout: Moves developed system into the production environment for access by users. Also includes end-user training, setting up a help desk, defining support procedures, and loading historic data so that the system is ready for live use.	*End-User / Administrator Documentation* *Training Materials*
Live Use: System is used "live" for the first time.	
Post Rollout Review: Surveys users to ensure the system meets the defined need.	*Project Sign-off Document*

activities is risky. For example, omitting user acceptance testing may result in an unusable system when it goes online. A risk like this is not worth taking. The adage is true: Organizations never seem to be able to make the time to implement a project properly, but they always can make the time to implement it again when it goes wrong.

This book does not provide details on project planning and management techniques, topics that can fill a complete book by themselves. However, some key activities for controlling a CPM implementation are included as part of this chapter.

Specifications

Many projects fail because there was not a well communicated and understood set of requirements at the start of the implementation. An inaccurate specification typically manifests itself during the project as a constant debate over what the project is intended to deliver. At the end of the project, the result of an inaccurate specification is a system that is unlikely to solve the original problem, will cause other issues to arise, will be considered a failure, and will need to be reimplemented at additional cost.

For a CPM application, the specification stage may take longer than any other stage. Although modern-day software solutions can be implemented in a fraction of the time of older systems, the time needed to specify requirements is not reduced. Assuming that the project scope has been accurately completed, five items will need to be specified in detail:

1. *The CPM data model.* Clarify what information is to be held and the associated business rules. The model is specified in terms of data stores, business dimensions, organizational structures, currencies, measures, and any calculated variables such as ratios and allocations.
2. *User work flow.* Determine how users will interact with the system. The user work flow describes how users will be led through the affected processes and the information they will need to complete a task.
3. *Reports and analyses.* Describe in detail the reports, analyses, and alerts that the new system will generate.
4. *Data load formats.* Identify the different data sources and how they are to be integrated into the CPM data model.
5. *Security.* Spell out who gets access to the defined processes and data.

Acceptance Testing

Acceptance testing is a specific task that determines whether the developed solution meets the defined needs. These needs are defined either before the project begins or, at the latest, before the specification is complete. Acceptance testing should be performed in a formal manner and should encompass six components:

1. *Arithmetical accuracy.* Verify that a known, accurate set of results is generated from a known set of input data.

2. *Appearance.* Confirm that data entry layouts, reports, and analyses are as specified.
3. *Work flow.* Check that menus appear in the correct and logical sequence for each process.
4. *Control.* Ensure that the system allows the right people to perform the right processes and access the right information.
5. *Performance.* Assess whether the system performs within the boundaries specified at the start of the project. For example, verify that the budget cycle from data collection to review can be achieved within one working day if that is what was specified.
6. *Usability.* Review the system as a whole and ensure that it works in accordance with the user and administration guides.

Record all acceptance-testing results. For any item that fails the testing, create an action plan to correct it or determine whether it is necessary to realign the specification with the resulting system.

Training and Support

Training for administrators, budget holders, managers, and support staff is something that must happen before the solution goes live. Training will be required in a number of areas including:

- Goals of the new system and how it will aid competitiveness
- Changes to the organization's business processes and any related terminology
- How users will benefit from the new system
- How to use the system
- How to obtain help and support

To train their employees, one organization set up a special room in which system users worked during the first few weeks after the system went live. Here they could access the system and complete their tasks but had immediate access to the development staff who helped them work through any issues that arose.

Two types of implementation support are needed. The first type relates to processes. The support staff must know about the organizational processes as well as how the system carries them out. The second type of support relates to machines and accessibility problems. The support team must be prepared and educated. If it is not, users who encounter problems—even those of their own making—will soon become disillusioned with the process and system. Bad experiences can sour the benefits and hopes that were expected of the new system.

Information Technology Involvement

Most packaged financial applications, including CPM systems, are designed to be set up and maintained by the finance department. Typically, administration users are given simple-to-use facilities for maintaining the data model, business rules, data entry screens, reports, and analyses. In essence, everything they need to accommodate changing business requirements is provided.

However, CPM systems involve many people and cut across departmental boundaries. As a result, they rely heavily on the supporting IT infrastructure. For this reason, IT must be involved in the project. Its active involvement is required in a number of ways:

- Providing the appropriate hardware/software environment for development and production use
- Loading and maintaining access to the application software, data model, and associated user interfaces
- Performing the initial setup of the database workspace
- Providing user access security over and above that delivered by the application; this usually is related directly to the technology being used and typically involves database and web access security
- Ensuring users have the appropriate communication links to the application
- Extracting data from any transactional systems in accordance with the agreed-on formats for loading it into the application
- Tuning the database and network for performance once the application has been created
- Providing application and database backup
- Providing end-user technical assistance

Project Control

The CPM direction team needs to meet regularly to monitor progress of the CPM implementation. Each team member should take responsibility and be able to report on the area for which he or she is accountable. The discussions, actions, and conclusions of these meetings should be recorded and distributed as appropriate.

During CPM implementations, project specifications and deliverables do change. There is no point in delivering a solution that does not meet real requirements. All potential changes that arise should be reviewed using an agreed-on change control procedure that includes documenting the change and circulating it to each member of the CPM direction team. Team members then should assess the impact on their area of responsibility.

Where possible, changes should be saved for a future phase of the implementation. Where they are to be included in the current phase, however, revised specifications and project plans will need to be generated and circulated to all members of the development team. Should a change cause the project to go outside the terms of the original business case and project scope, the project should be suspended until those terms can be adjusted and the project replanned.

Continuous Communication and Education

Another element of controlling an implementation involves never assuming that everyone knows what is going on or knows how to use the resulting system. Within the enterprise there will be staff turnover. Therefore, a continuous program of education and training should be established. One way to accomplish this is through scheduled formal training sessions. Another way is through informal methods such as newsletters and web-based training solutions.

Software firm Computer Associates (CA) initially trained 150 people when its CPM system went live. For the second pass they trained 250 more people. Today more than 700 people have access to the system. Carl Caputo, finance director at CA, commented, "We want everyone to be aware of the information and to be able to manage it."[1] The training sessions revealed some unexpected responses at CA. When asked how people reacted to the system during training, Caputo reported, "We were surprised. People really embraced the new responsibility and they wanted input. We got so much eager participation—it was really encouraging."

Whatever form training takes, materials should be prepared knowing that most users are not accountants. Use terminology that is easily understood by anyone. Make training to the point and relevant. By educating users and informing them of the business benefits, the organization is more likely to achieve user acceptance of the system and associated processes.

Overcoming Organizational Resistance

Because they involve so much change, CPM projects will incur resistance from within the organization. This resistance needs to be dealt with; it will not dissipate on its own. Resistance can come from all levels of the organization, but it is particularly serious when it comes from senior managers and others who can affect the success of the CPM initiative. The organization can do five things to minimize the occurrence and effects of this resistance.

1. *Secure senior management sponsorship of the project.* From the outset, the CPM project must be seen as having senior management sponsorship and full endorsement. Members of the project team must have and be seen to have the delegated authority of the senior management team and must, where necessary, have access to any person in the organization.
2. *Communicate objectives and benefits.* The project must be publicized among those who will be impacted in clear, concise, forward-looking documents that outline the short- and long-term objectives and the business benefits that will be gained from the solution. Other methods of communication could include presentations by the chief executive officer or other senior managers, videos, e-mail, newsletters, and more. Whatever method or combination of methods is used, the communications must emphasize that the solution is strategic in nature and an essential system that will help individuals meet organizational objectives.
3. *Bring known issues—and detractors—into the open.* When the proposed solution has influential skeptics and detractors, bring the skeptics together with key supporters so that the issues can be properly discussed in the open. This meeting should have an agreed-on agenda that outlines the issues in advance. Comments and action points raised in the meeting should be documented and followed up. Recognize that, quite often, detractors can be turned into supporters by involving them in defining requirements to solve business issues. Ensuring the system does something for them specifically in a first release can help emphasize the benefits of the CPM initiative.
4. *Never make it personal.* Although detractors may have a personal agenda, comments and actions should not be targeted at them personally. Instead, the business benefits of the CPM initiative

should be reemphasized. Also emphasize the likely results of not doing anything at all.

5. *Build a sense of ownership.* The purpose of a CPM system is to make the organization more competitive and enable individuals to play a part in that success. Progress toward those goals needs to be communicated on a regular basis so that everyone knows this is not just a passing fad. Eliciting feedback from the different user communities can help generate this sense of ownership.

SUMMARY

Like any software implementation, CPM implementations need to be planned. Given the high-profile nature of a CPM solution, the way in which these projects are communicated, managed, and delivered will affect the way in which users view the system. All CPM systems are strategic in nature and have the potential to dramatically impact corporate performance. As such, they need senior executive support, the right software and hardware environment, and the right level of business, technical, and project management skills all aimed at implementing and monitoring strategy. "To implement a CPM system, you need buy-in and commitment from the top-levels of the organization, the courage to challenge existing practices, and an openness to new ideas," comments Greg Ponych, principal finance officer—budget at Brisbane City Council. He adds, "Most importantly, you need to understand the business processes you're trying to support with the technology."[2]

These projects should never be considered to be someone's "part-time" job. The software requirements or effort that will be needed to deliver a solution should not be underestimated. But these systems, when implemented correctly, do deliver real business benefits.

Endnotes

1. Interview with Carl Caputo, finance director, Computer Associates, August 2, 2002.
2. Interview with Greg Ponych, principal finance officer—budget, Brisbane City Council, July 22, 2002.

CHAPTER 10

What Lies Ahead

COMMUNICATING VALUE

Global accounting scandals and changes. Increased shareholder scrutiny and demands. Geopolitical unrest. The days of smooth sailing in the corporate world seem to have disappeared—if they ever really existed. Consider the impact these changes have had on the tenure of chief financial and chief executive officers in recent years. In 1990, an article in *CFO Magazine* noted that CFO turnover among the Fortune 500 was approximately 12 percent per year. In 1998, less than a decade later, it was 26 percent. Earnings surprises, bad news, failure to deliver on promises, unsound investment decisions, and poor strategy execution were some of the reasons for this increase.[1] In a similar article, it was estimated that in 70 percent of the cases where CEOs had failed, the cause was simply bad execution.[2]

As discussed throughout this book, the ability to execute strategy has become increasingly important. It signals the organization's ability to add value for its shareholders. Because of this need, CFOs and finance professionals are no longer operating as backroom record keepers. They are emerging as boardroom strategists, full partners in driving strategy and adding value to their organizations. According to the authors of *eCFO*, finance professionals of the future will spend more time "anticipating industry restructuring, proactively identifying opportunities, justifying investments based on the value they will offer as options in the future, and then creatively managing these options as a portfolio."[3] With technologies in place to eliminate the need for CFOs and finance personnel to spend time performing the repetitive, transaction-based, and non-value-added activities of the past, this vision is fast becoming a reality.

When companies and their executives *do* execute their strategies, however, a problem still may exist. Consider that in the industrial age, the worth of a company was accurately represented as tangible assets on the balance sheet. Assets typically included such things as buildings and machinery. Today, however, the value of many enterprises is generated primarily from intangible assets, including such things as brands, patents, leadership, research and development, customer loyalty, copyrights, partnerships, employee knowledge, and other revenue-generating entities and activities that traditional accounting methods fail to capture. Consider the value of Steve Jobs's leadership to Apple Computers, the brand worth of Starbucks, the impact of good processes on the success of FedEx, and the value of masterful supply chain management to Wal-Mart.

Depending on which study is read and what measures are used, anywhere from 30 to 97 percent of an organization's worth—its ability to execute—may not appear on its books. The authors of *Cracking the Value Code*, for example, found that by 1998, the book value of publicly traded U.S. companies was on average only 28 percent of their market value.[4]

Finance professionals and the accounting industry face enormous challenges in correcting this situation and communicating their full value to their stakeholders. First they must answer some basic—but controversial—questions. For example, what intangibles should be reported? In what way should they be defined? How should they be reported?

In his book *Intangibles,* Baruch Lev identifies three broad categories of intangibles (discovery and learning, implementation, commercialization) that he believes provide insight into an organization's ability to create ongoing value and outlines a "value chain scoreboard" that highlights nine areas of information he feels would be relevant in providing insight for investors, analysts, and others. Before such a system could be implemented, however, Lev acknowledges that a necessary first step in recognizing an organization's value creation capabilities would be to have a policymaking organization, such as the Financial Accounting Standards Board, standardize a reporting structure for the description of information related to the intangible assets and investments, and carefully define the valuation criteria.[5]

Even if such a standardization were imperfect and allowed a range of results, Boston-based research and consulting firm Aberdeen Group believes that "the relative value of an intangible—as compared to industry competitors when using the same valuation method, for example—still provides critical decision-making information that is not currently available. A downward trend in a company's intangibles—e.g., its customer base—puts investors on notice that future sales revenue may be in jeopardy."[6] A second, even more daunting challenge that many professionals feel is long overdue is an overhaul of generally accepted accounting principles (GAAP). This, however, is a subject for another book.

A third challenge will be to locate and implement technology that has the architecture and business intelligence to accommodate accounting for intangibles. Unfortunately, many software vendors offer systems based exclusively on GAAP, which means they will not be able to make the transition to fair value accounting without significant architectural redesign.

According to Aberdeen Group, fair value accounting will require expansion beyond GAAP. One requirement, for example, will be the need for technology solutions to accommodate continuously changing asset valuations. Additionally, vendors "will need to define the business rules that logically express the interrelationships between the financial touch points in fair value, such as the link between ongoing marketing expense on branding."[7] There also will be new metrics and best practices for this new accounting regime.

Investors are searching for ways to identify the companies best able to cope with the demands of the business world in the 21st century. A CFO who is willing and able to identify, measure, and communicate intangibles will obviously provide a more complete picture of the company's worth to the investment community. Reporting the value of intangible assets will make a company that is reporting positive results even more attractive. Fair value accounting will provide a company that must report negative results an opportunity to communicate how all its assets are being used to produce positive results going forward.

One of the driving forces behind the need to report on intangibles is the sheer number of individual investors who entered the market with the emergence of discount online brokers, such as Charles Schwab. These investors are demanding more meaningful information regarding how public companies plan to create sustained value for them. A second driving force, according to Lev, is "externalization," or the outsourcing of decision making from corporations to, for example, customers (tell Dell which features to include in your computer), suppliers (manufacturers managing distributors' inventories), and alliance partners (partners sharing research and development decisions).[8] These entities require more and better information than ever before. Today's information technology is making this possible by delivering a connected world.

CONNECTED WORLD

In his book *The Agenda,* author and business thinker Michael Hammer states his method of predicting major shifts in the business landscape and technology: " 'The Next Big Thing' often extends 'The Last Big Thing.' " He states that the last big thing, occurring in the 1990s, was the integration of processes and the demolition of internal business boundaries ("walls") through solutions such as enterprise resource planning. He predicts that the extension of that in the 2000s will be the "destruction of walls *between* enterprises."[9] Corporate performance management (CPM) certainly comprises processes within the enterprise, but it also will extend beyond the organization's borders to include customers, partners, and suppliers.

Extensible Markup Language (XML) and the Internet are breaking down these barriers, making communication between enterprises easier. Ratified by the World Wide Web Consortium (W3C) in 1998, XML is a platform-independent, royalty-free, universal format for structuring and sharing data across the Internet. It gives meaning to information through the use of easily understandable, user-defined tags and is very flexible. For example, the tag "<p>" in <p>500</p>, could be defined by an organization to mean price, people, paragraph, or anything else it wanted. XML can be used to present data on any device, including desktop computers, web TVs, cell phones, answering machines, personal digital assistants, and more.

Extensible Business Reporting Language (XBRL) is a relatively new XML-based framework for improving the ease of preparing, publishing, and exchanging financial information. Companies employing XBRL agree to use a common set of tags, which enables the comparison of one financial statement to another. They use XML style sheets to present information in specific formats. Currently XBRL International reports that Morgan Stanley, EDGAR Online, Reuters, Microsoft, Daimler-Chrysler, UK Inland Revenue, the U.S. Federal Deposit Insurance Corporation (FDIC), and every lending institution in Australia reporting to the Australian Prudential Regulatory Authority use XBRL to report financial information.[10]

How does XBRL make information more usable and easier to share? Consider this example. Traditionally, if one computer sent another computer data on a company's $5,000,000 in revenues, the number 5,000,000 would be transmitted. The receiving computer had to be programmed in a way to recognize the number, then had to place the number in a predefined bin called "revenues," and had to ensure that the bin was expecting figures in dollars, not pounds or yen.

With XBRL, the number is sent along with a label that indicates the number represents revenues measured in U.S. dollars. The sender standardizes the information but recipients can view it in any way they choose. The highly labor-intensive requirement to map the sender's data in to the receiver's analytical program goes away. It costs less for a receiver to "consume" a sender's message. Less time is spent on translation and data collection, information is easier to use and analyze, and financial communities benefit from more transparency in financial reporting.

Another tool that has been developed recently is Extensible Business Reporting Language General Ledger (XBRL GL). Its purpose is to smooth the collection, structuring, and communication of any information required for U.S. and European accounting, such as that found in general ledger systems, charts of accounts, journal entries, and more. Based on XML, it is system independent, chart of accounts independent, and reporting independent. XBRL GL is one way organizations might be able to more easily consolidate information from multiple systems, both from within the organization (many operating units, many companies) and without.

XBRL GL could have three effects on today's organizations.

1. It could make it easier for organizations with legacy systems to upgrade to today's more robust CPM systems, allowing these enterprises to finally have easy, on-demand access to critical business data.
2. Because information can be more easily shared, XBRL GL could pave the way for organizations to outsource mundane, repetitive functions once performed by their finance departments. The finance professionals could now spend more time analyzing the business, making strategic decisions, and adding value to the organization.
3. XBRL GL could signal the end for vendors trying to sell solutions containing closed, propriety interfaces. Open standards are here to stay.

In addition to XML, XBRL, and XBRL GL, a new computer technology model is being developed to make it easier for companies to share not only data but also applications. It is called XML Web services.

Microsoft, with its .Net platform and tools, is a leading advocate of this technology. As envisioned by technology professionals, XML Web services will act as a universal translator, allowing organizations to talk to one another and share data and programs easily even though they use different platforms, applications, and computing devices. Furthermore, once these XML Web services applications are built, they could be reused. More succinctly, everything will be able to talk to everything and everybody will be able to talk to everybody—easily.

Consider this example. An airline offers consumers the opportunity to purchase plane tickets online. It recognizes that its customers also might want to rent a car and reserve a hotel room as part of their travel plans. The consumer would like the convenience of only having to log on to one system instead of three, saving time and effort. The same consumer also would like to input personal information only one time instead of three times. The airline does not have car rental and hotel reservation systems in place, nor does it have any easy way to interface with potential car rental and hotel partners even though these businesses would all benefit from working together. To provide these services today requires the creation special programming, links, and systems by the airline and its prospective partners. It can be done, but it is not easy—nor is the work reusable.

Companies using XML Web services would rely on industry standard processes to build applications that would allow all these businesses to work together easily over the web. The services would allow the airline site to find and access the car rental and hotel reservation sites. The consumer would not see the communications among the multiple sites. All the consumer would see is that it is now possible to purchase a plane ticket, rent a car, and reserve a hotel room at one site—and fill out the personal history information (name, address, phone, etc.) only once. All three businesses would benefit by having an easy way to communicate with one another, and the consumer would have an improved experience.

Furthermore, these programs could be reused for other partnerships. For example, the hotel could offer its room reservation program to amusement parks, sports organizations, and other businesses for use on their web sites. A company might rent its services to another company, or it might provide the application free of charge in exchange for the exposure to potential new business. These programs would not have to be rewritten or reconfigured for these new business partnerships.

As proposed today, XML Web services are made up of four components.

1. *The Internet.* It is fast, efficient, and affordable.
2. *UDDI* (universal description, discovery, and integration), an XML-based Internet registry, helps businesses find each other. UDDI offers a framework for Web services integration.
3. *XML.* XML allows organizations to share information.
4. *SOAP* (simple object access protocol). SOAP allows organizations to conduct business with each other. It is a common protocol for enabling programs to call each other and return responses, regardless of the operating systems used at either company. SOAP uses HTTP (hypertext transfer protocol) and XML to perform its function.

XML Web services—and any platform that enables the sharing of applications and data between and among enterprises—will raise many technical issues regarding security, reliability, quality of service, payment tracking, and accountability (who is at fault if the application fails). Perhaps a bigger question from a business strategy perspective, however, is: What will the organizational impact be if everyone can easily connect to everyone? How will it impact the way the organization does business—or does not do business? What will it mean to the organization's industry as a whole? How will it affect the way the organization looks at partnerships and vendor relations? How will the competition use the technology to gain advantages in the marketplace?

CLOSING THE GAP BETWEEN FINANCE AND INFORMATION TECHNOLOGY

In a Robert Half International survey, 27 percent of financial executives said their greatest challenge today is keeping up with technology.[11] As businesses rely more and more on technology as a strategic tool, a need for a closer relationship between business representatives and information technology personnel continues to emerge.

Unfortunately, the relationship between finance and information technology within many organizations historically has been strained.

Businesspeople often feel that information technology (IT) does not understand the business issues. Finance does not understand the reasons why complex IT initiatives come in late and over budget. They lament that IT solutions do not deliver the expected results. At the same time, IT professionals have long bristled at being the invisible stepchildren within organizations, cut off from decision making and strategy and constantly under pressure to cut costs and people.

Market intelligence and advisory firm IDC recognizes the gap between business strategy and IT strategy, and has defined four stages of the IT/business relationship. The first is an "uneasy alliance," where IT is viewed as an efficiency tool and the technology executive has little connection with the rest of senior management. In the second stage, "supplier/consumer relationship," IDC notes that IT has a strategic plan that is related to corporate strategy, but IT still is not valued as a strategic tool. The third level IDC defines is that of "co-dependence/ grudging respect." At this level, there is some recognition that IT is a strategic tool, and the chief information officer is becoming more knowledgeable of cross-functional business processes. In the final stage, "united we succeed, divided we fail," a single strategy exists that incorporates both business and IT.[12]

As a partner in driving strategic solutions, the CFO or business representative will be responsible for making certain that IT understands the business needs of proposed projects. The IT department will need to make sure the business representative understands how proposed solutions will or will not impact the business and its strategy. In addition, once purchasing decisions have been made, both disciplines will need to continue to work together to ensure that the business problems are solved and that strategy can be successfully executed, monitored, and adjusted.

SUMMARY

In an article titled "Organizing to Create Value," David P. Norton states: "'Value' has become synonymous with 'intangible,' which embodies far more than financial management." He goes on to question who should own the value creation process within the organization and suggests that while CFOs have the general skill set to perform this function, few seem to be doing it. He suggests that a new role might emerge at the executive level to meet this challenge: chief value officer (CVO).[13]

Regardless of who fills this role, today's business professionals—like the early space explorers—live in an age that is both terribly exciting and terribly dangerous. Executives (and organizations) who develop and demonstrate strategic (financial and nonfinancial) thinking, understand how to apply technology to impact the organization's strategy, and add value and communicate that value to shareholders will be able to bridge the gap from strategy to execution.

Endnotes

1. Stephen Barr, "You're Fired," *CFO Magazine,* April 1, 2000.
2. Ram Charan and Geoffrey Colvin, "Why CEOs Fail," *Fortune,* June 21, 1999.
3. Cedric Read, Jacky Ross, John Dunleavy, Donniel Schulman, and James Bramante, *eCFO* (Chichester, U.K.: John Wiley & Sons, 2001), vi.
4. Richard E. S. Boulton, Barry D. Libert, and Steve M. Samek, *Cracking the Value Code* (New York: HarperCollins, 2000), 13.
5. Baruch Lev, *Intangibles* (Washington, DC: The Brookings Institution, 2001), 105–127.
6. Aberdeen Group, *Market Viewpoint: Can Financial Analytics Deliver Fair Value?* November 5, 2001, 6.
7. Ibid.
8. Lev, *Intangibles,* 108.
9. Michael Hammer, *The Agenda* (New York: Crown Business, 2001), 166–167.
10. XBRL International, *XBRL Faq,* www.xbrl.org/Faq.htm, August 19, 2002.
11. Robert Half International Inc., "Time Bandits" (press release), November 1, 2001.
12. IDC, *IT/Business Alignment: Is It an Option or Is It Mandatory?* January 2002, White Paper, Group Vice President, Solutions Research, Jan Duffy.
13. David P. Norton, "Organizing to Create Value," *BSC Online Member's Briefing,* April 2002.

APPENDICES A–G

Interactive appendices, consisting of a Microsoft Word-based series of templates and checklists that organizations can download and use to implement their own CPM vision, can be found at www.wiley.com/go/strategygap (password: Strategy).

INDEX

DATE DUE

JUN - - 2016			

Demco